SINGER

SEWING REFERENCE LIBRARY®

More Sewing for the Home

Cy DeCosse Incorporated
Minnetonka, Minnesota

SINGER

SEWING REFERENCE LIBRARY®

More Sewing for the Home

Contents

Also available from the publisher: *Sewing Essentials, Sewing for the Home, Clothing Care & Repair, Sewing for Style, Sewing Specialty Fabrics, Sewing Activewear, The Perfect Fit, Timesaving Sewing*

Library of Congress
Cataloging-in-Publication Data

More Sewing for the Home.

(Singer Sewing Reference Library)
Includes index.
1. Sewing. 2. House furnishings.
I. Cy DeCosse Incorporated. II. Series.
T1715.M67 1987 646.2'1 87-24556
ISBN 0-86573-235-3
ISBN 0-86573-236-1 (soft)

Distributed by: Contemporary Books, Inc.
Chicago, Illinois

CY DE COSSE INCORPORATED
Chairman: Cy DeCosse
President: James B. Maus
Executive Vice President: William B. Jones

MORE SEWING FOR THE HOME
Created by: The Editors of Cy DeCosse
Incorporated, in cooperation with the
Singer Education Department. Singer is a
trademark of The Singer Company and is
used under license.

Managing Editor: Reneé Dignan
Senior Art Director: William B. Jones

Art Director: Lisa Rosenthal
Writer: Gail Devens
Editors: Rita Opseth, Susan Meyers, Bernice Maehren
Sample Supervisor: Rita Opseth
Fabric Editor: Michele Joy
Technical Photo Director: Bridget Haugh
Sewing Staff: Phyllis Galbraith, Bridget Haugh, Ray Arndt, Sr., Kathy Davis Ellingson, Wendy Fedie
Photographers: Tony Kubat, John Lauenstein, Mark Macemon, Mette Nielsen, Rex Irmen, Graham Brown

Production Manager: Jim Bindas
Assistant Production Manager: Julie Churchill
Production Staff: Janice Cauley, Joe Fahey, Carol Ann Kevan, Yelena Konrardy, Christi Maybee, Dave Schelitzche, Linda Schloegel, Cathleen Shannon, Jennie Smith, Greg Wallace, Scott Winton, Nik Wogstad
Consultants: Ray Arndt, Sr., Peggy Bendel, Stephanie Carter, Diane Eliason, Kathy Davis Ellingson, Amy Engman, Zoe Graul, Kate Halverson, Pam Hastings, Judy Lindahl, Margaret Lourie, Lynn Marquardt

Contributing Manufacturers: Clotilde; Coats & Clark; Conso Products Co.; Dritz Corporation; Dyno Merchandise Corporation; EZ International; Gosling Tapes; June Tailor, Incorporated; Kirsch; Olfa Product Corporation; Pellon Corporation; Seams Great Products, Inc.; The Singer Company; Stacy Industries, Inc.; Swiss Metrosene, Inc.; Waverly Division of F. Schumacher & Co.
Color Separations: Spectrum, Inc.
Printing: W. A. Kreuger (1187)

How to Use This Book

More Sewing for the Home adds to your decorating skills by providing a helpful planning and coordinating guide. You can use the items in this book individually to enhance your existing decor, or by coordinating fabrics, you can make these ideas work together throughout your home.

The book is divided into four main sections. First, we start with a basic plan just as a professional designer does. In the second section, we proceed to window treatments, with ideas for any room in the home. The bedroom and bath have very special decorating needs, so ideas for these rooms are grouped in a separate section. In the final section are some techniques to apply from one project to another and ideas for accessories that can add that finishing touch.

Start with a Plan

The first section shows you the steps to take to set up a home decorating plan; included are decorating guidelines and designer tips for your plan. Whether you are sewing a simple accent, redecorating an entire room, or starting a new home, you will want to keep this overall decorating scheme in mind.

To achieve the style or effect you want in each room, you are encouraged to use your personal taste to select fabric and furnishings to sew. You'll enjoy sewing to create a tailored, cozy, special, or cheerful atmosphere, or whatever mood you decide is best for a room. Keep a decorating notebook, and collect samples of fabric, wallcoverings, and accessories that coordinate with your purchases. Learn as much as you can about fabrics: how to mix prints and colors, how to select the appropriate fiber and finish for the project, and how to clean and care for the finished item.

Windows First

When you think of sewing for your home, one of the first considerations is a window treatment. Since custom draperies and curtains are always a favorite, window measurements probably take priority in your decorating notebook. Instructions in *More Sewing for the Home* include professional workroom techniques. Select from pinch pleated draperies, bishop sleeve curtains, hourglass curtains, reverse roll-up shades, and tent-flap curtains. The window treatment you choose will make a major contribution to the overall effect of the room, from classic to contemporary.

Many contemporary window treatments, such as vertical blinds and shades, can be softened with a padded cornice or a valance. A fabric-covered cornice coordinates with draperies or curtains but works equally well with shades or blinds. You can use a soft valance, such as a pouf or double pouf, by itself or in combination with another window fashion. Tapered valances can be soft or formal; so can swags and jabots. Swags and jabots originated as a traditional style, but updated versions are often more relaxed and casual.

Around the House

The bedroom and bath are often decorated to coordinate with each other. Sew a duvet cover and dust ruffle with shams to match. Then coordinate these with a shower curtain, embellished towels, and a sink or vanity skirt. A padded headboard can be impressive; yet with the instructions included in this book, this accessory is not as difficult as it looks.

Welting, trimmings, and ruffles can add professional-looking detail to items that you sew, so we tell you how to apply them to projects. Boxed cushions are an ideal finishing accessory; the step-by-step instructions can be followed to make a new pillow or cushion or to re-cover a chair, sofa, or bench cushion. Fabric screens, vertical blinds with fabric inserts, and upholstered walls require little sewing but truly coordinate the decorating plan of a room.

Projects to Sew

At the beginning of each project is an overview followed by cutting directions. For easy reference, fabrics and notions required to complete the project are included in a box labeled "You Will Need." In most cases, measurements are necessary to determine how much fabric is needed, so study the cutting directions to estimate the fabric needed. When you know the width of the fabric you will be using, you can accurately determine how much fabric to buy.

The instructions given are complete; you do not need to purchase additional patterns. The colorful photographs that accompany the instructions show you how the project should look at each step of its construction. Contrasting thread is sometimes used so the sewing technique shows clearly in the photo; for your own projects, however, you will usually want to use matching thread.

Step by step, project by project, *More Sewing for the Home* shows you how to accomplish your decorating plan. With the help of its guidelines and techniques, you will be able to turn your decorating ideas into beautiful home fashions.

Sewing with a Plan

You are the decorator when you sew for your home. The prospect can be as overwhelming as planning and coordinating the window treatments, pillows, and accessories for an entire new home, or it can be as simple as selecting a fabric for a kitchen curtain. Often, however, the single sewing project becomes only a beginning for a project to refresh or update a whole area of the house.

Start by looking at your decorating needs and sewing projects room by room. A home generally looks larger and more pleasing when colors and patterns flow easily from one room to the next. Colors and patterns should relate, but they may branch off into different color schemes and moods. Devise a plan for your sewing project as a whole, but then work at it step by step. Any project will look smaller when broken into smaller pieces.

Where to Start

Most designers start planning the color scheme and direction for a home with the first rooms that are seen. The entry and the living room are usually these focal points. If the dining room is connected to the living room, look at the entry, living room, and dining room as one unit when considering colors and moods.

From the dining room you may move into the second area, the kitchen and family room, and sometimes the utility room and a related bathroom. A separate look or mood may coordinate these rooms, but the colors and fabrics you select should be compatible with the colors you have selected for the living and dining rooms. If the kitchen joins these first two areas of the home, it should be compatible, too.

The third area, the master bedroom and bath, is another distinct area that has a special mood. Bedrooms are personal areas that are more apt to have fabrics and colors that reflect your personality, tastes, and interests. The remaining bedrooms and baths for children or guests may have another color and fabric direction. A guest bedroom may do double-duty as a sewing room, home office, or den.

Record Keeping

An important part of the sewing plan is a notebook with pocket folders so you have a place to collect samples and swatches. Organize your notebook into the four general areas of the home. Leave plenty of pages between sections for all the information you

will collect for each room. Clip pictures and fill your notebook with ideas. Look for a mix in fabrics and colors, and interesting uses of texture and trimmings. The more ideas you collect for each room, the better.

Keep window measurements, room plans, pictures, and snapshots for each room in this notebook, along with phone numbers of important resources. A sturdy tote bag can be used for carrying heavy, bulky samples.

Sources of Ideas

For inspiration, save magazine pictures of rooms that you like. Some classic styles remain stable year after year. It is often the detailing of trims, colors, and fabrics that can update home furnishings.

Many designers keep design magazines and trade publications that will also give you ideas. Furniture stores, model rooms, and catalogs have photos of window treatments, pillows, and accessories that you can sew. Most major cities have model homes and showcase houses that show the newest in decorating trends. Wallcovering books are also inspirational sources of decorating ideas; they show ideas for mixing fabric prints and using borders and stripes.

Using a Decorator or Designer

Although you are the one planning and sewing for your home, you may still want to use the services of a designer or decorator to help you with your fabric and decorating decisions.

Retail fabric stores that specialize in fabrics for home decorating usually have a *decorator* or *decorating consultant* to help you select appropriate fabrics, trims, and sewing accessories. This person can also help you select fabrics that go together, estimate how much fabric you need, and advise you on special sewing techniques for the fabric.

A *designer* is trained to go beyond putting together colors and patterns. Designers are problem solvers who work with line, form, color, texture, direction, pattern, and unity and composition within a room or home.

Through a designer you may be able to have a greater choice of fabrics than what is available in a retail store because designers have access to the fabric collections that design professionals use. They usually charge for services only if purchases are not made through their sources. They are often basic "do-it-yourselfers" so they understand when you want to sew a project yourself, but a designer may not be able to help you with sewing problems.

Design Considerations

Line. In addition to the lines created by furniture, consider all the lines in a room, such as moldings and beams, chair rails, and flooring. When selecting a window treatment, use a simple curtain rod if a decorator rod will create too many additional lines in a room.

Color. Don't forget to think of the tone of the woodwork and the color of fireplace brick when choosing fabric and carpet colors to blend with a room.

Texture. Dressy fabrics and casual fabrics usually have contrasting textures. Velvets and rough, nubby textures do not mix in the same room. Heavy-textured plaid upholstery fabrics do not mix with silky, sheer balloon window treatments.

Pattern. The more pattern in a room, the more country-like and traditional the room feels. Several patterns may work effectively in a room, but quieter, simple tailored fabrics may be more pleasing for longer lengths of time.

Direction. The focus, or direction, of a room may be a fireplace wall, a piece of art, a view, or a conversation area. Use fabric and color to help focus or coordinate the area.

Unity and composition. A room with a "put-together" feeling has unity and composition. It is often a successful mixing of the old with the new. This style, called *eclectic*, is the most difficult to achieve because there are so few rules. As an example, to make a room more interesting you may use contemporary fabrics and colors with traditional antiques and country furniture.

TIPS FROM A DESIGNER

Update a room at minimal cost with one new fabric repeated two or three times around the room; for example, use the same fabric for a valance, tieback panels, and pillows.

Add interest quickly and easily with two exciting new fabrics to re-cover chair cushions, a bench cushion, a window seat, or a table covering.

Mix patterns and furniture styles. Contemporary fabrics are acceptable on traditional furniture; traditional fabrics are acceptable with contemporary window treatments, such as mini-blinds and louvered shades.

Change a fabric if a room feels heavy instead of light and airy. Avoid using too many small prints of the same scale in the same room.

Warm up a plain, conservative room with a splash of color. Make some new pillows, or add a new side panel or valance treatment to traditional draperies.

Creating an Atmosphere

List five words that you and your family would use to describe the results you wish to achieve from your decorating. These words will evoke different feelings about color, fabric patterns, and texture as well as furniture design and shape. For a family room or kitchen you may think of sunny, bright, clean, crisp, and cheery — or rich, warm, mellow, cozy, and traditional.

Elegant, comfortable, or traditional might be appropriate for the living-dining area. Strong, masculine, and rustic might be words for a library, den, or bath. Contemporary, clean, spacious, and

dramatic might be words for a bedroom. For someone else the mood for a bedroom might be romantic, soft, plush, feminine, and comfortable.

In the photo above, beige, gold, and pink tones suggest elegance. Fabrics with subtle sheen accent the mitered stripes on pillows, the softly shirred Austrian valances, and the fabric rosette. Simply changing a color or fabric can change the feeling in the room and create a different overall effect of the decorating. Use the chart on the opposite page to get you started with your own decorating ideas.

Guidelines for Decorating

Overall Effect	Suggested Colors	Fabrics & Textures	Items to Sew
Elegant, special, or refined	Refined colors: mauve, taupe, gold, metallic, ecru	Shiny fabrics or fabrics with sheen: silks, fine cottons, antique satins, moires, rayon trims	Mitered pillows (pages 14, 23), swags & jabots (pages 52, 62), Austrian valances (page 58), rosettes (page 109)
Comfortable, casual	Autumn colors: rust, tan, gold	Smooth to lightly textured finishes, no scratchy finishes: polished cottons, chintzes, warp sateens, casements	Turkish floor cushions (page 23), cloud valances (page 56), welted pillows (page 110)
Cozy, restful	Soft to medium shades: blue, mauve, green	Softly padded or quilted fabrics, inviting prints: cotton sheetings, warp sateens, chintzes	Duvet covers (page 74), tuck-pleated shams & dust skirts (pages 78, 80), daybed covers (page 86), padded headboards (page 90)
Practical	Multi-colors, medium shades: red, blue, orange	Washable or stain-resistant fabrics, overall prints: sheetings, cotton blends	Tapered valances (page 60), duvet covers from sheets (page 82), vertical blinds with fabric inserts (page 120), fabric screens (page 122)
Conservative, clean & neat, tidy, crisp	Light colors, warm tones: white, mauve, peach, ecru, maize	Fabrics with woven designs, nubby textures, allover prints: sheer linens, cottons, casements	Pinch pleated draperies (page 34), hourglass curtains (page 44), padded cornices (page 66), reverse sham bedcovers (page 84)
Tailored, masculine	Earth tones, rich colors: rich rust & brown, intense blue & green	Geometrics, plaids, stripes: upholstery fabrics, tapestries	Mitered pillows (pages 14, 23), flanged shams (page 22), reverse roll-up shades (page 46), tent-flap curtains (page 50), boxed cushions (page 114)
Cheerful	Bright, clear colors: pink, yellow, blue, green, orange	Bold florals & stripes, fabrics with contrasting colors: decorator cotton prints, warp sateens	Tent-flap curtains (page 50), cloud valances (page 56), reverse sham bedcovers (page 84), shower curtains (page 94), fabric screens (page 122)
Romantic	Fresh colors: pastel pink, blue, green, peach, ivory	Fabrics that encourage touching: silks, polished cottons, sateens, florals, water-color prints, laces, eyelet borders	Pouf valances (pages 54, 55), ruffled duvet covers (pages 76, 77), duvet covers from sheets (page 82), padded headboards (page 90), tieback shower curtains (page 94), rosettes (page 109)
Contemporary	Neutral tones: beige, gray, ivory, cream	Textured or smooth fabrics: simple designs, solids, casements	Reverse roll-up shades (page 46), tent-flap curtains (page 50), padded cornices (page 66), piped duvet covers (page 74), welted pillows (page 110), vertical blinds with fabric inserts (page 120)
Traditional, classic	Reliable colors: green, white, blue, burgundy	Timeless fabrics: antique satins, jacquards, matelassés, linens, velvets	Pinch pleated draperies (page 34), hourglass curtains (page 44), swags & jabots (pages 52, 62), boxed cushions (page 114)

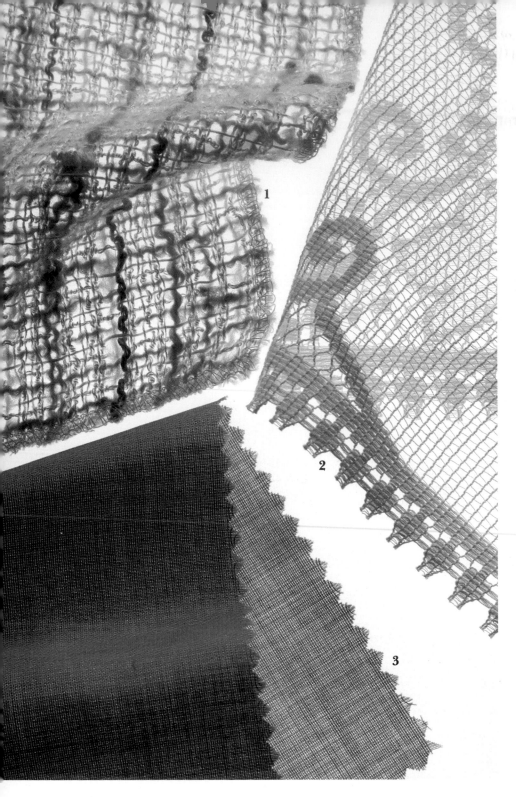

Fabric Selection

It pays to use good quality fabrics for home decorating projects. A good quality decorator fabric usually lasts longer and results in a finer finished look. Some of the most popular home decorator fabrics are shown here and on the next pages to help you with your selection.

As a rule, the tighter the weave or higher the thread count (number of threads per inch), the stronger the fabric. Most decorator fabrics have a higher thread count than garment fabrics.

Many decorator fabrics have a stain-resistant finish. To test, drop a small amount of water on the sample. If the water beads up instead of soaking in, the fabric will repel stains. This is more of a concern for cushions, pillows, slipcovers, and upholstery than for window treatments. Also, make sure that the dyes do not rub off when the fabric is handled or rubbed between your fingers.

Consider the end use, and be sure that the fabric is appropriate to the function. A decorative top treatment for a curtain, for example, will receive little wear; if a simple style is selected, it can be changed easily to update a look. Fabric for such a project does not get the heavy use that a chair cushion does; nor is it used as long as the average drapery. Remember that the average drapery may hang in a room anywhere from eight to fifteen years.

When comparing costs for large amounts of fabric, consider that prints may cost more than solid fabrics because you will need more fabric to match the motifs. The larger the repeat, the more likely you are to waste fabric when matching.

Lightweight open weaves are often used for window treatments because they let in the sunlight yet offer more privacy than undraped windows. Casement fabrics (**1**) are loosely woven, with uneven yarns and open areas. The variation in the weave creates a design in the fabric. Polyester, cotton, or linen fibers may be used. Laces and eyelets (**2**) may look delicate and fragile, but are easy to sew and provide a light, airy look. Wide borders and finished edges eliminate hemming. Sheers (**3**) vary in fiber content but are usually polyester for a sheer, transparent look. Imported sheers can be up to 118" (295 cm) wide with embroidered or decorative hems.

Fiber Content

Cotton is a basic, strong, all-purpose fiber for home furnishing fabric. It dyes well for vibrant colors and has good wearability. It may be used as a blend with many other fibers.

Linen is strong, but it will wrinkle. If wrinkling is a concern, crush a handful of fabric tightly in your fist and release it to see if wrinkles are retained. Decorator fabrics usually do not have crease-resistant finishes.

Rayon and acetate are often used together or in blends for a rich, silky appearance. Acetate may stretch in draperies and may spot if it gets wet.

Polyester is used alone or combined with other fibers to add stability. With all synthetics, use a low iron temperature when pressing.

Decorator Fabric vs. Garment Fabric

Decorator fabrics can be more expensive than garment fabrics, but garment fabrics may not have all the features you need. Normally, garment fabrics are not treated with stain-resistant finishes, and they usually have a lower thread count so they are not as durable. Use garment fabrics if the item will get little or no wear and your goal is simply to create an effect. Some garment fabrics are not heavy enough for a drapery, but may be acceptable as a curtain, valance, or dust ruffle.

If using garment fabric, preshrink it. If repeated washing will be necessary for an item, do not sew it with materials that cannot be washed, such as buckram or linings.

Mediumweight basics are versatile multipurpose fabrics used for window treatments, cushions, cornices, and fabric screens. Chintz (1) is a glazed, plain-weave cotton or cotton-blend fabric. This tightly woven fabric is available in solid colors or prints that are often large, traditional florals. Warp sateen (2) is a cotton or cotton blend that has a softer hand than chintz but feels heavier. Warp threads float on the surface to create a smooth surface. This fabric is multipurpose for draperies, bedspreads, cushions, and slipcovers. Antique satin (3) varies in fiber content and quality. It is a very drapable, mediumweight solid fabric, which has slubs and a sheen.

Sailcloth and duck are medium to heavyweight plain-weave fabrics in cotton or cotton blends. They have a matte finish, without the sheen of chintz or sateen, so they have a more casual appearance in either solids or prints.

Upholstery fabrics are generally durable and long lasting. Available in a variety of textures and fiber contents, they include nubby linens, napped nylon velvets, and smooth cottons.

Preview Fabrics at Home

When shopping for fabric, take along samples from the room, such as an arm cover from a sofa, pillows from a chair, carpet samples, wallcoverings, and paint chips. These samples will help you select what you will take home to preview. Colors are very difficult to remember without samples for matching.

When looking at fabrics in the store, set aside the ones that blend well with your samples and remove those that do not. Select several fabric samples to take home.

Because of the difference in lighting, fabric may not look the same in your home as it does in the store. Store lighting is usually all or part fluorescent, whereas home lighting is usually natural or incandescent. To see how a fabric looks in a home environment, look at it in daylight and under home artificial light.

When you get home, drape the sample close to or on the area where it will be used. Keep it there for at least 24 hours to see if you like it. If the colors do not work or you dislike the pattern, this trial period will help you select something on your second outing that is closer to the effect you want. If you have a lot of solid colors in your room and want to switch to a print, the room will become more active. Make sure that the fabric sample you take home is large enough to show the pattern and the effect it will have on the room.

If you are attempting to match a solid color, be aware that dye lots can vary from the sample. If a close match is necessary, be sure there is enough fabric on one bolt for the project or that other bolts have the same dye lot. When you order from a swatch, request a cutting of the current dye lot for approval before the goods are actually shipped.

Fabric Care

When selecting fabrics for home decorating, consider the colorfastness, durability, and care required. Check the manufacturer's recommended cleaning method. This information may be printed on the selvage or on the end of the fabric bolt. The salesclerk should also be able to provide the care information for you.

When choosing drapery fabrics, keep in mind that you will need to be tolerant of small fluctuations in the length of draperies after you hang them. No fabric is completely stable; the looser the weave, the less stable the fabric. Looser weaves are also more affected by heat and moisture; in humid climates the hemline in a loosely woven drapery can rise and drop in length more than one made from a tightly woven fabric.

If the manufacturer recommends drycleaning, the fabric should not be washed. Washing can soften buckram headings and linings; it can also shrink the trimmings, linings, and decorator fabric differently.

Although draperies do not get as much wear as upholstery and carpeting, they are subject to sun fading and deterioration from dust, heat, and moisture. Water spotting on draperies is usually a problem for drycleaners to remove, so try to prevent rain stains.

It is recommended that draperies be cleaned after the pollen season for health reasons, especially if you or someone in the household has allergies. Draperies may need cleaning less frequently if dust is regularly removed and stains are immediately treated. The most effective way to protect draperies from dust is to be sure that windows are sealed tightly, because dust and pollen coming into your house from outdoors become trapped in your draperies. Changing or cleaning the filter on a forced-air furnace frequently will also protect fabrics in your home from dust.

To extend the life of your draperies, vacuum them periodically. Dust may also be removed by tumbling drapery panels for a few minutes in a clothes dryer without heat. Be sure to remove drapery pins before tumbling window treatments in the dryer. To prevent wrinkles, remove the drapery panels from the dryer as soon as it stops.

Also vacuum upholstered pieces regularly to prevent dust from accumulating on the fabric surface. Rotate cushions regularly to ensure even wear and to keep cushions from breaking down and becoming lumpy. Upholstery is always cleaned intact.

Many decorator fabrics are treated with a stain-resistant or water-resistant finish. If the item gets obviously soiled, it can be spot-cleaned in place with an appropriate stain remover for the fabric. The protective finish should be reapplied after laundering or drycleaning. You may do this yourself with a spray, available from retail stores. Or a drycleaner can usually apply the finish for you.

No fabric will withstand strong exposure to the sun; however, a good-quality drapery lining will help protect draperies from sun fading. Keep lined draperies closed to prevent fading of carpet and upholstery. Even with care, colors will naturally fade over a period of time. If fading is a concern, sun films with ultraviolet filters can be applied directly to the window glass.

Mixing Patterns

There are six basic categories of patterns in fabrics, and any decorating plan may use several of them in the same room. All six patterns can be used effectively in one room if you have a balance of color along with pattern size and scale.

TIPS FROM A DESIGNER

Four to six different patterns tend to become eclectic.

Less pattern mix is often more contemporary in feeling.

Repeat one strong-patterned print at least once or twice in the room. For example, a strong print in a sofa could be repeated in a valance. If both areas are on the same side of a room, you could also cover a chair, bench, or cushion across the room.

Mini-prints can be overdone. Do not repeat more than two mini-prints in the same area, including wallcoverings. If you use two mini-prints, their scale could be different and the colors reversed.

Compare the outfitting of a room with personal tastes in clothing. Several prints, colors, and textures can be worn together, but colors must be coordinated effectively, textures must feel right together, and there must be an accent or a point of interest.

Repeat strong accent colors more than once.

Have fun. Do not be afraid to let fabric and colors reflect your personal taste. Take time to find out what your tastes and style preferences are. Then carefully follow the step-by-step process for decorating success.

Solids are often used in flooring, carpeting, walls, wallcoverings, and window treatments.

Geometric prints, such as checks and plaids, are not strictly for sporty looks. Many soft, silk-like fabrics have treated finishes and can be used in living rooms for a casual, elegant look. As chair coverings and throw pillows, they blend well with other textures.

Medallion patterns are usually small in scale and are often used in wallcoverings and in fabrics for chairs and pillows.

Stripes in subtle colors are often used in casement draperies and foyer wallcoverings; bolder stripe patterns may be used on chairs and sofas.

Overall prints and florals are most easily used on larger pieces, such as sofas and chairs, or major areas, such as draperies and valances.

Combination prints use two or more of the above patterns, and look best when used in larger areas, such as sofas, draperies, valances, and accent pillows.

Borders, Stripes & Wide Fabrics

Fabrics with borders or wide stripes have many possibilities for coordinating color and design within a room. By removing a border from one fabric and applying it to another, or applying it in an unusual way, you can create an entirely new fabric. You can also manipulate striped fabrics to change their appearance by using them diagonally, mitering to the center, or cutting them apart to create a border on a coordinating fabric.

Estimate the amount of border that it will take for the project or decorative effect. It is possible to get several yards of border from a few yards of striped fabric cut into strips. Doing this is usually more economical than buying a bordered fabric. When cutting the stripes, allow ½" (1.3 cm) seam allowance on each side of the stripe for application.

Railroading Wide Fabrics

To eliminate seams, *railroad* a fabric. To railroad a fabric, turn the fabric on its side so that the normal width of the fabric becomes the length. This technique can often be used on valances, cornices, and dust ruffles, but is particularly practical for short curtains and seamless sheer draperies when fabric is extra wide.

The advantage of making draperies without seams is that there is no unevenness or puckering where widths of fabric are joined. In sheer fabrics, having no seams has the additional advantage of eliminating shadows at the seams. Railroading may require less fabric, and it saves time because there are no seams to sew.

Coordinate bedroom accessories with bordered sheets and pillowcases. Miter the border from a sheet for a flange edge on pillow shams. Also use the border to trim a neckroll pillow.

Use a border or a stripe as a boxing strip or insert on Turkish cushions.

Use a border or a stripe to coordinate tiebacks with draperies.

Miter stripes to meet at the center of a pillow.

Appliqué a border on a solid fabric for banding on edges of shades.

Window Treatments

Measuring Windows

After deciding on the window treatment, install the appropriate hardware and then measure for curtains, draperies, shades, or top treatments. You will be determining the *finished length* and *width* of the treatment. To determine the *cut length* and *width*, add the amounts needed for hems, casings, seams, matching repeats, and fullness. Fill in a copy of the chart right. Suggested hem allowances for the projects in this book are given in the Cutting Directions specific to the project. Use these measurements to estimate the amount of fabric needed. Pinch pleated draperies require special measurement considerations for determining length and width and estimating fabric (page 35).

Use a folding ruler or metal tape for measuring; cloth tapes may stretch or sag. Measure and record the measurements for all windows separately, even if they appear to be the same size.

Special Measurement Considerations

Allow ½" (1.3 cm) clearance between the bottom of the drapery and the floor when measuring for floor-length draperies. This amount allows for cleaning and vacuuming, and provides sufficient clearance for electric cords. Also, if draperies sag or if floors are uneven, draperies will not drag on the floor.

Allow 1" (2.5 cm) clearance for loosely woven fabrics. This amount will provide an extra margin for them to stretch slightly without dragging on the floor.

Allow ½" (1.3 cm) clearance on sliding glass doors; more than this amount may let light gap at bottom.

Allow 4" to 6" (10 to 15 cm) drapery clearance above baseboard heaters for safety.

Allow 2½" (6.5 cm) clearance if carpeting is not installed. This amount provides approximately 2" (5 cm) for carpeting and padding, plus ½" (1.3 cm).

Underdraperies should be 1" (2.5 cm) shorter, ½" (1.3 cm) at top and bottom so they do not show under the outer draperies.

Use the highest window in the room as the standard for measuring if windows are at different heights. Place all other draperies in the room at the same height from the floor.

Estimate Yardage

Cut Length	in. (cm)
For fabrics *not* requiring pattern match	
1) Finished length	
2) Bottom hem (double for most fabrics)	+
3) Casing/heading	+
4) Cut length for each width or part width	=
For fabrics requiring pattern match	
1) Cut length (figure as above)	
2) Size of pattern repeat (distance between motifs)	÷
3) Number of repeats needed*	=
4) Cut length for each width or part width: Multiply size of repeat by number of repeats needed	
Cut Width	
1) Finished width	
2) Fullness (how many times the finished width)	×
3) Width times fullness	=
4) Side hems	+
5) Total width needed	=
6) Width of fabric	
7) Number of fabric widths: Total width needed divided by width of fabric*	
Total Fabric Needed	
1) Cut length (as figured above)	
2) Number of fabric widths (as figured above)	×
3) Total fabric length	=
4) Number of yd. (m) needed: Total fabric length divided by 36" (100 cm)	yd. (m)
For wide sheers, which can be railroaded	
1) Finished width times 3 (fullness)	×
2) Number of yd. (m) needed: Total width needed divided by 36" (100 cm)	yd. (m)

*Round up to the nearest whole number.

NOTE: Add extra fabric for straightening ends.

NOTE: Half of the width will be used for each curtain panel. To piece panels, adjust width measurement to include 1" (2.5 cm) for each seam.

Determine Cut Length

Measure from the top of the rod to the desired length. To this length measurement, add the amount needed for lower hems, rod pockets, headings, and pattern repeat.

Lower hems. Add double the desired hem to finished length. For mediumweight fabrics, use a 4" (10 cm) double hem on floor-length curtains or draperies; add 8" (20.5 cm) to the length. For sheer and lightweight fabrics, a deeper double hem of 5" to 6" (12.5 to 15 cm) may be used. On short curtains or valances, use a 1" to 3" (2.5 to 7.5 cm) double hem.

Rod pockets and headings. For rod pockets with no heading, add an amount equal to the diameter of the rod plus ½" (1.3 cm) to turn under and ¼" to 1" (6 mm to 2.5 cm) ease. The amount of ease depends on the thickness of the fabric and the size of the rod. Lightweight fabrics require less ease; rod pockets for large rods require more. For rod pockets with headings, use the formula for a rod pocket, adding to it an amount twice the depth of the heading.

Pattern repeat. Prints must match across the width of the panels. Measure the distance between motifs, and add that amount to the cut length of each panel.

Determine Cut Width

To the finished width, add the amount needed for seams, side hems, and fullness.

Seams. For multi-width panels, add 1" (2.5 cm) for each seam. Panels that are not wider than the fabric do not require an extra amount for seams.

Side hems. Add 4" (10 cm) per panel for a 1" (2.5 cm) double-fold hem on each side of panel.

Fullness. Fabric weight determines fullness. For laces and medium to heavyweight fabrics, add 2 to 2½ times the finished width of the curtain. For sheer and lightweight fabrics, add 2½ to 3 times the finished width.

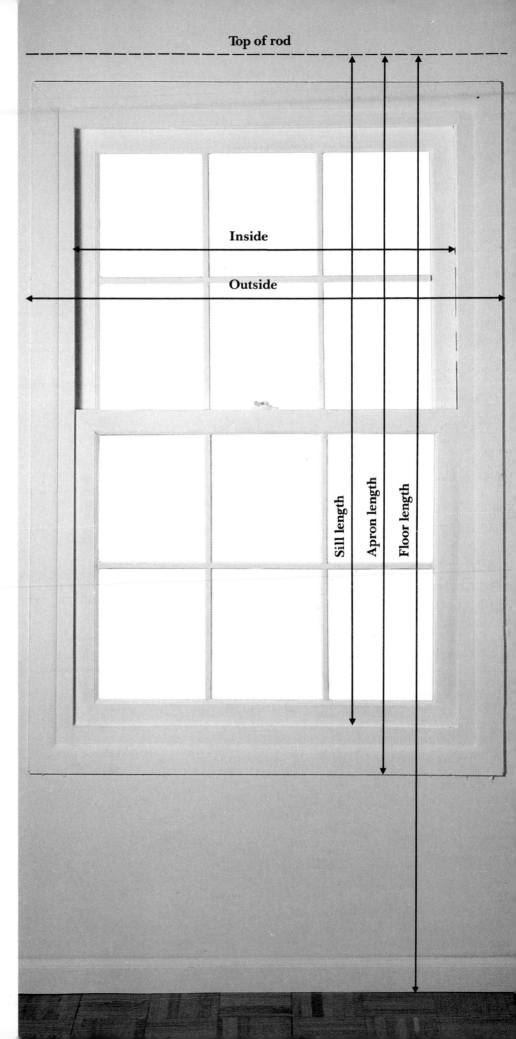

Top of rod

Inside

Outside

Sill length

Apron length

Floor length

Curtain & Drapery Hardware

Choosing hardware for your window treatment is as critical a decision as the window fashion. When selecting your window treatment, consider the effect of the curtain hardware.

1) Continental® rods are curtain rods that are deeper to add emphasis at the top of the curtain. They are available in two widths: 2½" (6.5 cm) and 4½" (11.5 cm).

2) Sash rods have ¼" (6 mm) clearance at ends and are used for shirred curtains on windows and doors. For an hourglass curtain on a door, use a sash rod at the top and bottom.

3) Clear plastic rods for sheer and lace curtains do not show through and detract from the fabric.

4) Single curtain rods are used for rod pocket curtains and stationary window treatments. These rods are available with a clearance of from 2" to 5" (5 to 12.5 cm). A special canopy rod has a clearance of 7½" (19.3 cm).

5) Double curtain rods consist of two rods with 1" (2.5 cm) difference in the clearance to hang a valance and a curtain on the same mounting.

6) Ringless decorator traverse rods for pinch pleated draperies have slides concealed in the rod for a clean, contemporary look. The top of the drapery skims the lower edge of the rod.

7) Unfinished wood pole sets, plain or fluted, can be painted to match the curtain fabric for a custom touch.

8) Decorative traverse rods are cord-controlled to open and close. Draperies are attached to rings that slide on a hidden track. These rods can also be used for layered treatments with underdraperies, curtains, or shades. Top treatments are not necessary because the brass-finished or wood-finished rod is decorative.

9) Cafe rods are used with clip-on or sew-on rings, or with casual tab-top curtains. A choice of finishes is available, including brass, enamel, and wood. Cafe rods and wood pole sets are used for hand-drawn window treatments. The curtain is opened by hand rather than a pull-cord.

10) Spring-tension rods are adjustable for inside mounting. Soft plastic or rubber tips hold rods securely in place without requiring screws or holes. Use round rods for shower curtains and cafe curtains, and flat rods for inside window casings and shower curtain valances.

11) Conventional traverse rods are used for draperies that open and close with a cord. They can open from the center or either side. Draperies hide the rods when the panels are closed, but these rods can be used with a stationary valance or cornice so the rod is concealed when the draperies are open. These rods also come in sets designed specifically for layered treatments.

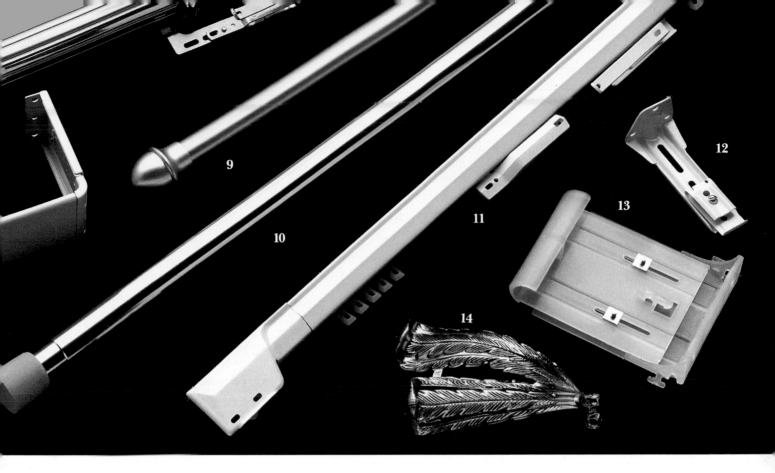

12) Support brackets should be placed every 12" to 20" (30.5 to 51 cm), depending on the weight of draperies. On multi-paneled windows, align brackets with the frame between panels.

13) Tieback holders fit behind the last fold of draperies to prevent crushing and to hold the folds in clean, graceful lines. The projection of the holder can be adjusted from 5" to 8" (12.5 to 20.5 cm).

14) Holdbacks have projection arms or stems used to hold draperies back from the window.

Basic Terms to Know

a) Drapery return is the measurement from the last pleat of the drapery panel to the wall.

b) Projection, or clearance, is the measurement from the wall to the back of the master slides.

c) Length measurement for conventional traverse rods is from end bracket to end bracket. For decorative rods, it is from end ring to end ring.

d) Master slides are attached to the draw cord to push or pull the leading edge of each drapery panel.

Overlap is the area where drapery panels overlap in the center of a two-way traverse rod. Standard overlap is about 3½" (9 cm) per panel.

Stackback is the amount of space occupied by open draw draperies. This space depends on the panel width, pleat spacing, and fabric bulk but is usually one-third the rod width. Allow for one-half the amount on each side of the window.

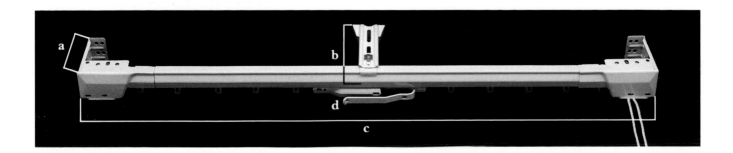

Matching Prints

Prints require careful planning. To avoid wasting fabric or making costly errors, cut, match, and stitch carefully. Prints must be positioned to please the eye, and they must be sewn to match at every seam. Start matching a print at eye level so if the match does become imperfect, it will be off at the top or bottom of the panel, where it is less noticeable.

Start a full print at the bottom of a curtain or panel. If the print is behind a sofa or piece of furniture, position a full print at the top of the furniture line.

Match motifs across drapery or curtain panels. Be sure that motifs on all curtain panels match at eye level when there are several windows in the same room or area.

Because most decorator fabrics have a stabilizing finish applied to the surface, it is not advantageous to pull a thread to straighten a crosswise end. Cut decorator fabrics at right angle to the selvages, or follow a printed motif.

Two Ways to Cut Crosswise Ends

Use T-square or right angle to straighten crosswise ends. Place the T-square or right angle parallel to selvage. Mark cutting line; cut on marked line with shears or rotary cutter.

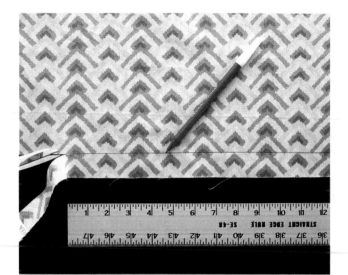

Follow a design line that runs across fabric on crosswise grain. Cut along design with shears or rotary cutter.

How to Match Prints Traditionally

1) Match motifs from wrong side by placing point of pin through matching designs. Pin at close intervals to prevent shifting.

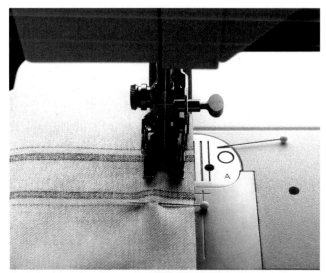

2) Stitch, using Even Feed™ foot to keep seam aligned. Remove pins as you come to them.

How to Match Prints As You Sew

1) Position panels with right sides together, matching the selvages.

2) Fold selvage back at top of panel until pattern matches on both panels.

3) Pin next to the fold at point where the design matches; turn fabric over to the right side to check matching. No other pins are necessary.

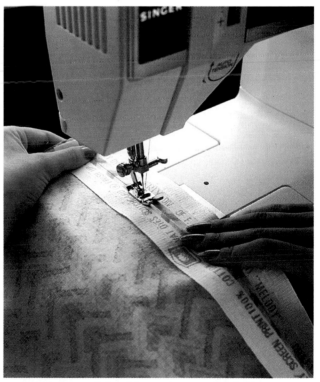

4) Stitch from right side as close to the fold as possible. Keep fabric taut while lining up motif as pinned. Continue sewing without additional pins, matching the motifs as you stitch. Trim off selvages.

Seams & Hems

How to Sew a French Seam

All seams in home decorating sewing are ½" (1.3 cm) unless otherwise indicated. When cutting fabric, remember to add the seam allowances to the finished size of the item you are sewing. Use a seam appropriate to the fabric when none is specified.

Avoid placing a seam in the center of wide items such as bedcovers, top treatments, or round table toppers. Split the panels and put the seams on sides so you will have a wide, full panel in the center. On cloud, Austrian, and pleated valances, hide the seams with a scallop or pleat.

Plain seams, stitched with right sides together and pressed to one side, are used if the item is to be lined. If the item is not lined, finish raw edges with a zigzag or multistitch zigzag. Or overlock the seam allowances together.

French seams are appropriate on sheer fabrics and unlined curtains, draperies, table toppers, and dust ruffles. Because all raw edges are enclosed, this seam is especially stable for washable items.

Overlocked or serged seams are timesaving and practical for home decorating because the seam is stitched and overedged at the same time. The overlock machine is a supplement to a conventional sewing machine.

Double bottom and side hems are standard for window treatments. The longer the panel and lighter weight the fabric, the deeper the hem should be. Use double 4" (10 cm) hems on curtains or draperies that are longer than window length. Be careful not to place a hem in front of the window; when light comes through the curtain, the hem or lining edges should not be visible. Double side hems are usually 1" or 1½" (2.5 or 3.8 cm).

1) Pin *wrong* sides of fabric together. Stitch a scant ¼" (6 mm) seam. Press seam allowance to one side.

2) Turn fabric panels so right sides are together to enclose trimmed seam allowance. Stitch ⅜" (1 cm) from folded edge, enclosing first seam. Press to one side.

Overlock Hems

Rolled edge sewn with 3-thread overlock stitch is durable and neat on lightweight fabrics. Use it on tablecloths, napkins, and ruffles that otherwise require narrow hem. Contrasting thread can be used for decorative detail.

Satin edge is sewn with short, narrow 3-thread or 2-thread overlock. This method is good on textured fabrics, because it is less bulky than rolled edge. Use woolly nylon thread for better coverage.

Overlock Seams

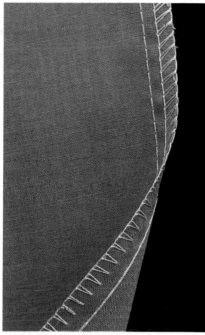

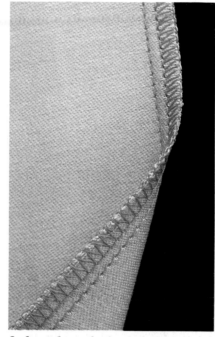

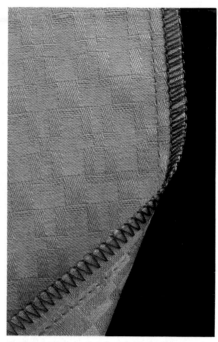

4-thread overlock seam is durable, nonstretch, self-finished seam. Use for long straight seams.

3-thread overlock seam is an alternative for 4-thread seam. Use with conventional straight stitches, if necessary, to reinforce and to prevent stretching.

2-thread overlock stitch is fast, neat technique for finishing plain seams or raw edges of fabrics that ravel. Edges may be overlocked either before or after seam is stitched.

How to Sew a Double-fold Hem

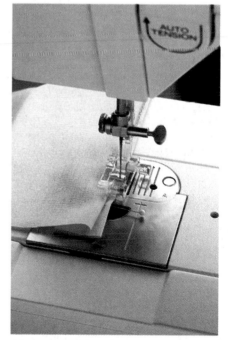

1) Turn under hem allowance. Press the fold. Turn under hem allowance again; press in place.

2) Straight-stitch on folded hem edge, using 8 to 10 stitches per inch (2.5 cm). When stitching several layers of bulky fabric, lighten pressure slightly and stitch slowly.

Alternative method. After pressing hem, fold back to right side, leaving a fold of fabric about 1/8" (3 mm) from hem edge. Set machine to blindstitch. Adjust zigzag stitch to take tiny bite.

Pinch Pleated Draperies

Pinch pleated draperies are a popular treatment for windows because draperies open to let in light, and close for privacy. The pleats are spaced at intervals to control the fullness of the drapery. The more fabric that is pleated into the drapery panels, the fuller the draperies become.

Although pleater tapes are a quick solution for some draperies, the fullness, spacing, and depth of the pleats are limited when you use these tapes. The only way to have total control over the fullness and position of the pleats is the traditional buckram heading used in drapery workrooms.

Before you can determine the size of the drapery panels, you must determine the hardware and the mounting. For conventional rods, measure from ½" (1.3 cm) above the top of the rod to the desired finished length. For draperies that are mounted on decorative rods, measure from the pin holes in the rod to the desired finished length.

Remember to include stackback when mounting the rods. This is the amount needed at the side of the windows for the drapery to clear the window when the drapery is open to its fullest. Actual stacking space will vary with the weight of the fabric, the fullness, and whether or not the drapery is lined, but it can be estimated at one-third the window width measurement. For center-pull draperies, allow for half the stacking space on each side of the window.

✄ Cutting Directions

Measure the window, and follow the guidelines for curtains and draperies (pages 26 and 27). There are two basic measurements to consider: finished length and finished width. Estimate yardage and cut the lengths for drapery and lining, using the chart on the opposite page. These directions are for a pair of draperies.

YOU WILL NEED

Decorator fabric for draperies.

Lining fabric for lined draperies.

Conventional traverse rod, ringless decorator traverse rod, or wood pole set.

Buckram, 4" (10 cm) wide, for heading.

Estimate Yardage

Drapery Length	in. (cm)
1) Window length as measured from rod	
2) 8" (20.5 cm) for heading	+
3) 8" (20.5 cm) for double hem	+
4) Cut drapery length	=
Drapery Width	
1) Rod width (from end bracket to end bracket on conventional rods; from end ring to end ring on decorative rods)	
2) Returns	+
3) Overlap [standard is 3½" (9 cm)]	+
4) Finished drapery width	=
Widths per Panel	
1) Finished width times 2, 2½, or 3 (fullness)	
2) Width of fabric	÷
3) Fabric widths needed: round up or down whole width	=
4) Divide widths by 2	÷
5) Number of widths per panel	−
Total Drapery Fabric Needed	
1) Cut length (figured above)	
2) Fabric widths (figured above)	×
3) Total fabric length	=
4) Number of yd. (m) needed: total fabric length divided by 36" (100 cm)	yd. (m)
Lining Length	
1) Finished length of drapery	
2) 4" (10 cm) for double hems	+
3) Cut lining length	=
Lining Width	
Number of widths per panel: For lining 54" (140 cm) wide, cut same number of widths as for drapery fabric. For lining 48" (108 cm) wide, one more width is usually required	=
Total Lining Fabric Needed	
1) Cut length (figured above)	
2) Fabric widths (figured above)	×
3) Total fabric length	=
4) Number of yd. (m) needed: total fabric length divided by 36" (100 cm)	yd. (m)

Drapery Pleats

Use the drapery pleat worksheet to determine the number and size of pleats and spaces per panel. The recommended amount of fabric required for each pleat is 4" to 6" (10 to 15 cm). The recommended space between pleats is 3½" to 4" (9 to 10 cm), approximately the same amount as the center overlap. If the worksheet calculation for the pleat size or the space between pleats is greater than the recommended amount, add one more pleat and space; if the calculation is smaller than the recommended amount, subtract one pleat and space.

Drapery Pleat Worksheet

Finished Panel Width	in. (cm)
1) Finished drapery width (figured left)	
2) divided by 2	÷
3) Finished panel width	=
Space between Pleats	
1) Number of widths per panel times number of pleats per panel*	=
2) Number of spaces per panel (one less than pleats)	=
3) Finished panel width (figured above)	
4) Overlap and returns	−
5) Number of spaces	÷
6) Space between pleats	=
Pleat Allowance	
1) Flat width of hemmed panel	
2) Finished panel width (figured above)	−
3) Pleat allowance	=
Pleat Size	
1) Pleat allowance (figured above)	
2) Number of pleats in panel	÷
3) Pleat size	=

*Figure 5 pleats per width of 48" (122 cm) fabric, 6 pleats per width of 54" (140 cm) fabric. If you have a half width of fabric, figure 2 or 3 pleats in that half width. For example, for 48" (122 cm) fabric, 2½ widths per panel = 12 pleats.

How to Sew Unlined Pinch Pleated Draperies

1) Seam widths together as necessary. (Remove selvages to prevent puckering.) Use French or serged seams. Turn under and blindstitch or straight-stitch double 4" (10 cm) bottom hems.

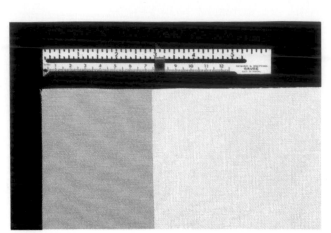

2) Cut 4" (10 cm) wide buckram 6" (15 cm) shorter than width of panel. On wrong side of drapery panel, place buckram even with top edge and 3" (7.5 cm) from the sides.

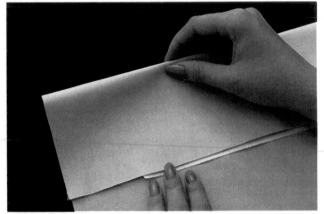

3) Fold heading over twice, encasing buckram in fabric. Press; pin or hand-baste in place.

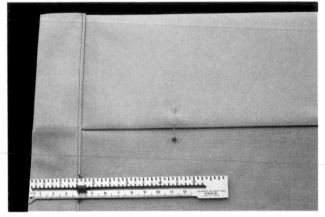

4) Turn under and blindstitch or straight-stitch double 1½" (3.8 cm) side hems. Determine size of pleat and space between pleats from worksheet (page 35).

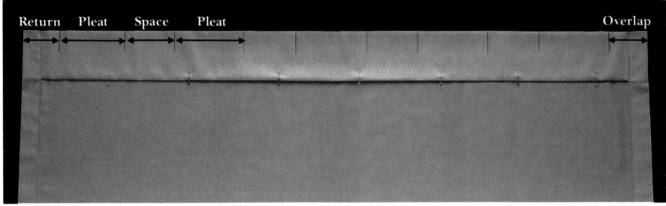

Return   Pleat   Space   Pleat   Overlap

5) Mark the returns and overlaps on each panel; then mark the pleats and spaces. Make sure there is a pleat just before the return and next to overlap. Pleat size can vary slightly to accommodate excess width, and pleats can be adjusted as necessary to hide seams in pleats. Keep the spaces uniform.

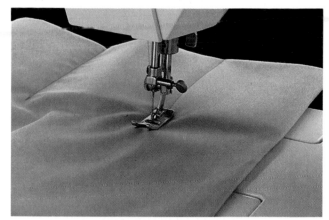

6) Fold individual pleats by bringing two pleat lines together and pinning. Crease buckram on the fold.

7) Stitch on pleat line from top of heading to ½" (1.3 cm) below heading; backstitch to secure.

8) Divide into three even pleats. Crease the fold of the pleat with one hand while opening the pleat at the top of the heading.

9) Press fold straight down to meet the pleat stitching line. Two pleats form at the sides.

10) Pinch outer folds up to meet center fold. Finger press three pleats together, making sure they are all even.

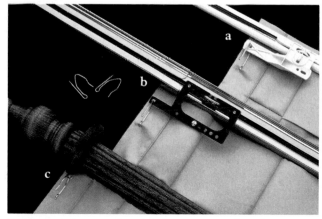

11) Tack pleats with machine bar tack in center of pleat, ½" (1.3 cm) from bottom of buckram. Set machine for widest stitch, and stitch 4 to 5 times.

12) Insert drapery hooks. On a conventional traverse rod **(a)**, top of hook is 1¾" (4.5 cm) from upper edge of drapery. On a ringless decorator traverse rod **(b)**, hook is ¾" to 1" (2 to 2.5 cm) from upper edge. On a wood pole set **(c)**, hook is ½" (1.3 cm) from upper edge.

How to Sew Lined Pinch Pleated Draperies

1) Stitch drapery fabric, following step 1, page 36. Sew lining widths as necessary, using plain or serged seams. (Remove selvages to prevent puckering.) Turn under and stitch a 2" (5 cm) double bottom hem.

2) Place drapery on table or large flat surface. Lay lining on top of drapery, with *wrong* sides together and hem of lining ¾" (2 cm) above the hem of the drapery.

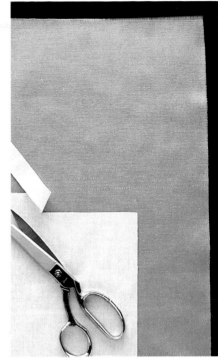

3) Trim 3" (7.5 cm) from each outside edge of lining. Trim lining so it is 8" (20.5 cm) from top edge of drapery.

4) Follow step 2, page 36. Then fold heading over *twice*, folding buckram over lining at the top. Press; pin or hand-baste.

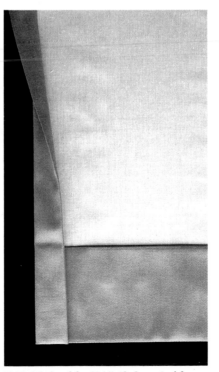

5) Fold double 1½" (3.8 cm) side hems over the lining.

6) Blindstitch side hems (page 33). Finish draperies, following steps 5 to 12, pages 36 and 37.

Dressing Draperies

Window treatments need hand-dressing, or training, to keep them looking their best and most attractive. Before hanging draperies, press them with a warm, dry iron to remove any wrinkles. After draperies are hung, if wrinkles still exist, press with a warm, dry iron over a hand-held roll of paper towels.

If fabric is particularly hard to train into pleats, you may want to finger press. Place the front edge of the drapery between the thumb and index finger, and follow the front edge of the pleat all the way to the hemline. Finger pressing creates a light crease and helps train the drapery and tailor the pleat.

Roman shades may also need to be raised and then tied in position for a few days to set the folds. Then when the shade is raised again after being lowered, the pleats will naturally fold into the right position.

How to Dress Draperies

 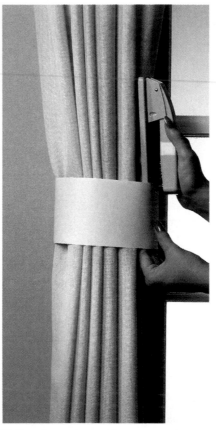 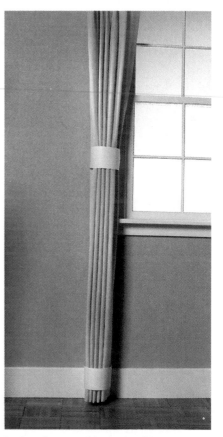

1) Draw draperies into the stacked position. Starting at top, guide pleats into soft folds. If lined, catch lining in folds. Make sure depth of folds is even. Use grain of fabric as guide to keep pleats perpendicular to floor.

2) Staple a piece of paper or tie a piece of muslin around the pleats halfway between top and hem to hold them in place. Do not fasten so tightly that wrinkles appear.

3) Staple second piece of paper at the hemline. The draperies should hang straight from the rod. Leave tied for 5 to 7 days. Humidity will encourage the setting process.

40

Tiebacks

Jumbo welting tiebacks are a versatile change from traditional straight or tapered tiebacks. They can be braided, twisted, knotted, or shirred to coordinate with drapery and curtain panels. Piped tiebacks with a shirred insert are perfect coordinates with the soft, puffy look of bloused curtains or lightweight tieback panels.

Placing a tieback low gives a visual effect of widening the window; place it high to add height. The most popular positions are approximately one-third or two-thirds of the window height, or at the sill. If cafe curtains are used under the draperies or curtains, the tiebacks are most often held back at the level of the cafe rods.

To determine how long to make tiebacks, measure around the curtain by holding a tape measure loosely at the height you want the tieback. Add 1" (2.5 cm) to the length for seam allowances.

You can also estimate that for a pair of draperies, a tieback is half the rod width, plus 4" (10 cm). It is generally not a good idea to tie back a drapery that is wider than it is long. If a drapery is tied back, it should remain tied back as a stationary panel; wrinkles and folds take several days to fall out.

How to Sew Braided Tiebacks

1) Cut cording 3 times the finished length of tieback; cut fabric strips 1½ times the length of tieback. Encase jumbo cording as on page 112, steps 1 to 3. Trim cording out of the ends; turn ends to inside, and slipstitch closed.

2) Overlap the three tubes slightly at one end. Hand-stitch tubes together, and braid. Cut other ends of tubes to desired tieback length; finish as for first end of tieback.

3) Use pin-on ring **(a)** or tack a curtain ring **(b)** in the center of each end. Attach rings to cup hook on the wall.

Jumbo Knotted Tieback

Cut cording 2 times the finished length of tieback plus 40" (102 cm) for knot. Cut fabric strips the length of tieback plus 20" (51 cm). Encase cording, page 112, steps 1 to 3. Tie big knot in center. Cut tieback to desired length. Trim cording out of ends. Turn ends to inside; slipstitch closed. Tack curtain ring on each end.

Jumbo Twist Tieback

Cut cording 2 times the finished length of tieback; cut fabric strips the length of tieback plus 1" (2.5 cm). Encase jumbo cording, page 112, steps 1 to 3. Trim cording out of ends. Turn ends to inside; slipstitch closed. Hand-stitch ends of tubes together, and twist. Tack curtain ring on each end.

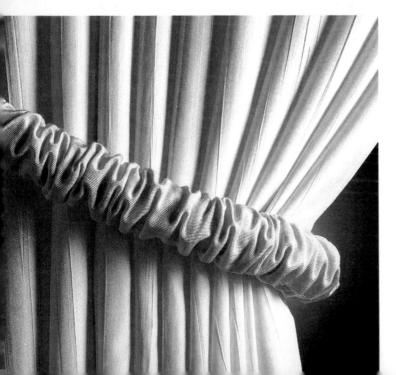

Shirred Jumbo Welting Tieback

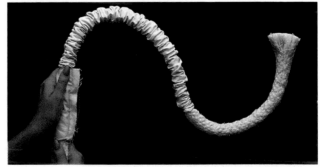

Cut cording 3 times the tieback length. Cut fabric strips 2 times the tieback length and 2" (5 cm) wider than circumference of cording. Fold strip around cording, *right* sides together. Encase cording, page 112, steps 2 and 3, gathering fabric as tube is turned. Finish ends; attach rings.

Shirred Insert Tieback

1) Cut insert 2 times finished length plus 2" (5 cm) and finished width plus 1" (2.5 cm). Cut lining 2" (5 cm) longer and 1" (2.5 cm) wider than finished tieback. Cut buckram ¼" (6 mm) narrower than finished size. Cut bias strips for welting (page 110) 2 times the finished length, plus 4" (10 cm) extra for finishing ends.

2) Gather both edges of the insert. Make welting (page 111). Machine-baste welting on right side of shirred strip in ⅜" (1 cm) seam. Pin right side of lining to right side of strip. Stitch ½" (1.3 cm) seam. Turn right side out.

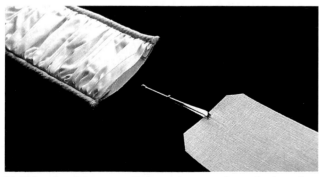

3) Trim buckram to slight point at one end. Attach bodkin to pointed end, and insert buckram between gathered insert and lining.

4) Trim 1" (2.5 cm) of cording out of welting at ends. Turn under a double ½" (1.3 cm) hem at ends, and slipstitch in place. Attach rings in center of tieback.

Hourglass Curtains

Hourglass curtains take their name from their shape. They are held taut between sash rods at the top and bottom of the window glass, and then pulled in at the center to create the hourglass shape. Use tension rods, instead of sash rods, for mounting inside a window frame.

Because these curtains are held tight to the glass, they are a practical treatment for doors. They also work well on windows where there is not room for a return. They allow sunlight to get in and, for extra airiness, are attractive in lace and sheer fabrics.

You will need to take two length measurements: the length at the center of the curtain and the *adjusted* length at the sides. The adjusted length accommodates the pinching in of the fabric at the center of the window. Estimate 2" (5 cm) extra at the sides for every 12" (30.5 cm).

✂ Cutting Directions

Cut the fabric 2 to 2½ times the width of rod. Cut the length as measured in step 1, right. Add allowance for rod pockets and headings at top and bottom of curtain plus 1" (2.5 cm) to turn under.

YOU WILL NEED

Lightweight decorator fabric for curtains.

Two sash rods or tension rods; mount rods before measuring.

How to Sew an Hourglass Curtain

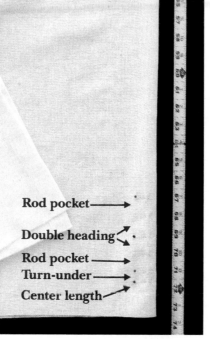

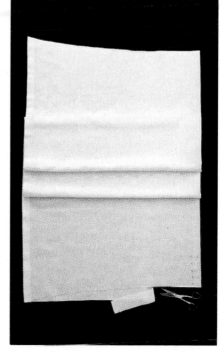

Rod pocket ——→

Double heading ——→

Rod pocket ——→

Turn-under ——→

Center length ——→

1) Measure for side finished length. With a tape measure or string, plan the curve of the hourglass shape on the door or window. The narrowest part of hourglass should be no less than one-third the width of the glass.

2) Turn under and stitch double 1" (2.5 cm) side hems. Fold panel in half lengthwise; on the fold, mark the center finished length, plus rod pocket and heading allowance. Be sure markings are equal at both ends of fabric.

3) Mark a gentle curved line from side length at hemmed edge to center length about 3" (7.5 cm) from center fold. Line should not have any curve at the fold. Cut on marked line at top and bottom.

4) Stitch rod pockets and headings at top and bottom of curtain. Insert sash rods.

5) Mount curtain. With string or tape measure, pull panel into hourglass shape at midpoint and measure for tieback. Add 2" (5 cm) for overlap. For tiebacks, see pages 41 to 43. To sew rosette, see page 109.

Reverse Roll-up Shade

The reverse roll-up shade is a practical, tailored shade covering the window frame and hanging from a rod inside a padded cornice. The contrasting lining that rolls to the outside of the shade is fused to the shade fabric.

Select two mediumweight, firmly woven fabrics that will bond well. Do not use fabrics that are water-resistant and stain-resistant. These fabrics are treated with silicone, which prevents bonding. Test a sample to be sure the fabrics bond securely. To prevent pattern show-through when sunlight comes through the shade, use a solid-color lining; light colors will also show sun fading less than strong colors.

The reverse roll-up shade goes to the sill, but because the lining is decorative, a portion of the shade is always rolled to the right side, even when the shade is lowered.

Make and cover the cornice, following the instructions on pages 66 to 69.

✂ Cutting Directions

Cut shade fabric and fusible web 1" (2.5 cm) narrower than inside measurement of cornice and 12" (30.5 cm) longer than length from rod socket in cornice to sill. Cut lining 2" (5 cm) wider and 3½" (9 cm) longer than shade fabric. Cut two lengths of shade cord, 3 times the length of the shade plus width.

YOU WILL NEED

Shade fabric, contrasting solid lining, and fusible web as determined at right.

Covered cornice, inside measurements 5" (12.5 cm) deep and 4" (10 cm) wider than window frame (page 67).

Four screw eyes, ½" (1.3 cm).

Utility rod with sockets, the same size as the inside cornice width.

One dowel, ½" (1.3 cm), width of finished shade; shade cord; awning cleat; drapery pull.

Note: If shade is wider than 36" (91.5 cm), add another angle iron, shade cord, and two screw eyes for center of shade.

How to Sew a Reverse Roll-up Shade

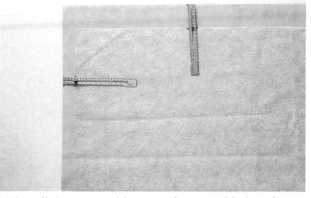

1) Place lining *wrong* side up on large padded surface. Center fusible web from side to side; position it 2" (5 cm) from one short end for top, and 1½" (3.8 cm) from bottom.

2) Place shade fabric *right* side up on lining, aligning edges with fusible web. Fuse the shade fabric to the lining, following the manufacturer's directions.

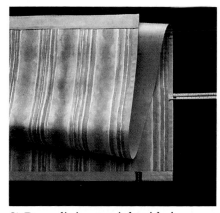

3) Press lining to right side in double ½" (1.3 cm) side hems; stitch. For rod pockets, press ½" (1.3 cm), then 1½" (3.8 cm) to right side on upper edge; press ½" (1.3 cm), then 1" (2.5 cm) to right side on lower edge; stitch.

4) Insert the dowel in the lower rod pocket; insert the utility rod in the upper pocket.

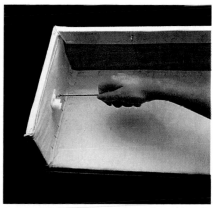

5) Mark center line along length of cornice top; insert screw eyes 2" (5 cm) on either side of center line and 6" (15 cm) in from ends. Attach curtain rod sockets to the center of cornice ends.

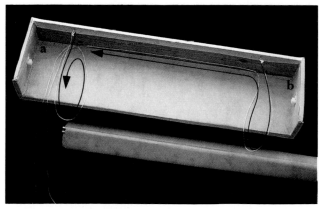

6) Tie cord on pull side (**a**) to screw eye at back of cornice, and thread through corresponding screw eye at front. Repeat for second side (**b**), bringing cord across top and threading through front screw eye on pull side. Mount cornice.

7) Attach awning cleat to side of window frame. Insert shade in sockets. Loop the cords around shade. Adjust cords so shade is level. Insert cord ends in drapery pull; knot ends.

Bishop Sleeve Curtains

These elegant pouffed curtains are simply rod pocket curtains with extra length allowed for blousing. The bishop sleeve look is achieved with tiebacks pulling the curtain tight to the window frame. Any number of poufs may be used. Arrange and tie the poufs at a position that is in proportion to the window length and width.

The poufs are balanced on each side of the tieback because the curtain rod extends 6" to 8" (15 to 20.5 cm) on each side of the window. If side space is limited, they may also hang straight on the outer edge, with the pouf draping only to the center of the window.

Tiebacks are tight on this curtain, in contrast to loose-fitting tiebacks on most curtain panels. For a decorative effect, use tasseled tiebacks or floppy bows with long streamers. Or use cord to tie the poufs so tiebacks do not show. As a finishing touch, the soft, flowing look of the bishop sleeve curtains can be repeated with pouf or cloud valances (pages 54 to 57).

✂ Cutting Directions

Cut panels 2 to 2½ times wider than finished width. To finished length, add 12" (30.5 cm) extra for each pouf and 12" (30.5 cm) more to puddle on the floor; add allowance for double top heading and rod pocket. Add 2" (5 cm) for double bottom hem if puddling on floor, or 8" (20.5 cm) for double bottom hem if curtains come to the floor.

YOU WILL NEED

Decorator fabric for curtains.

Tiebacks and cup hooks for each pouf.

Flat curtain rod or Continental® rod.

How to Sew a Bishop Sleeve Curtain

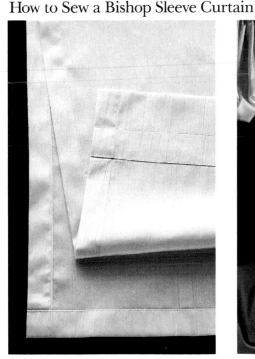

1) Turn under and stitch double 1" (2.5 cm) side hems. Turn under and stitch rod pocket and heading. Stitch double bottom hems.

2) Insert rod; hang and gather panels evenly. Determine location of poufs by tightly bunching the panel with your hands and lifting it to different positions until you find a pleasing proportion.

3) Mark tieback position. Attach cup hook behind pouf to hold tieback. Tissue paper can be tucked into the pouf to improve blousing if fabric does not have as much body as you would like.

Tent-flap Curtains

Stylish tent-flap curtains require a minimum amount of fabric and provide a tailored, uncluttered look. Choose two fabrics that complement each other for the outer fabric and the lining. The lining is just as important as the outer fabric.

✂ Cutting Directions

Cut each panel half the width of the mounting board plus return, plus 2" (5 cm) for seam allowances and overlap; cut length as measured from the top of the mounting board to desired finished length, plus the depth of the mounting board and ½" (1.3 cm) for seam allowance. Cut face fabric and lining panels the same size.

YOU WILL NEED

Decorator fabric and lining for curtains.

Mounting board: For outside mount, board should extend at least 1" (2.5 cm) on each side of window frame and be deep enough to clear window by 2" (5 cm). For inside mount, cut 1" × 2" (2.5 × 5 cm) to fit inside window.

Two tieback holders or two wooden blocks.

Two angle irons for mounting.

Heavy-duty stapler, staples.

How to Sew a Tent-flap Curtain

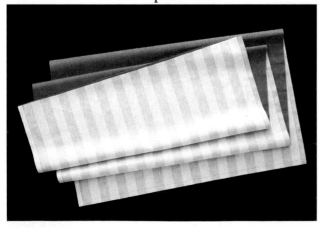

1) Pin face fabric to lining, right sides together, and stitch three sides in ½" (1.3 cm) seam, leaving upper edge open.

2) Press one seam allowance back to make it easier to turn a crisp, sharp edge. Trim seam allowance across corners. Turn panels right side out, and press.

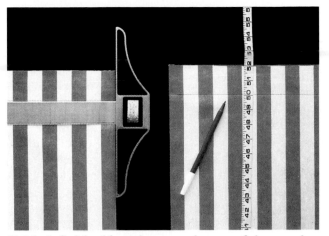

3) Mark finished length across the top of the panels, making sure that both panels are exactly even and that end is at perfect right angle to sides.

4) Align panel length marking with front edge of mounting board. Staple panel to board, starting at return. At corner, make diagonal fold to form a miter. Panels overlap about 1" (2.5 cm) at center.

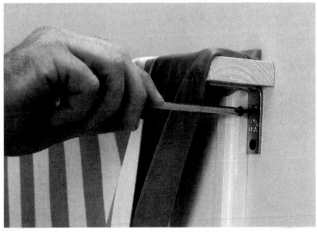

5) Mount board with angle irons positioned at edge of window frame.

6) Fold the front edges of the panels back to side edges, and adjust opening. Measure to be sure they are even on both sides.

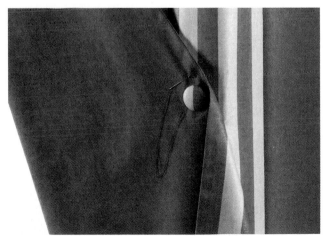

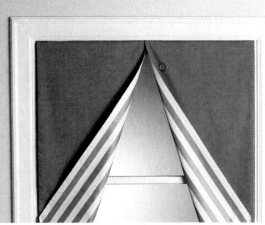

7) Hand-tack two layers together, and finish with decorative or covered button. Or hand-tack ties at front edge and sides. To maintain projection at sides, attach panel to tieback holder or wooden block attached to window frame behind ties.

Inside mounting. Cut panels half the finished width of mounting board, plus 1" (2.5 cm). Sew as for steps 1 to 3. Mount shade on front of board. Fold flap; tack to side of curtain. At side, sew ring to curtain back; attach to cup hook inside frame.

Top Treatments

Top treatments give curtains, draperies, or shades a custom look that sets the window apart from the ordinary. They include valances, poufs, swags and jabots, and cornices. They may be used alone, to allow the maximum light or view through a window, or with any curtain or drapery to cover an unattractive rod, or simply as a decorative accent.

Top treatments are used not only with curtains and draperies, but also with shower curtains, mini-blinds, pleated shades, vertical blinds, and shutters to soften the overall appearance or to coordinate fabric or color within a room.

A top treatment can be a useful camouflage. It can help to extend the visual height of a window or can make it appear shorter, depending on the style and placement. Valances and cornices can make windows that are at different levels in a room appear uniform. When wall space is limited for drapery stackback, a top treatment used by itself can give the window a finished look without a great deal of effort.

Fabric has a lot to do with the look. The same style can be made in moire or linen; the moire will be elegant for a tailored look, and the linen will be more casual for a country look. A straight valance or cornice is usually more tailored than one that is gathered, but in a formal fabric a gathered one can be just as elegant.

There are few hard and fast rules for top treatments, because they are an excellent opportunity to express creativity. In general, the length of the valance should be in proportion to the total length of the window or window treatment. This length is usually about one-fifth of the window treatment. To add visual height to a room, a top treatment may be mounted at the ceiling, or at least several inches (centimeters) above the window.

Valances are simply short curtains, draperies, or soft shades used at the top of a window. A valance may be mounted on a separate curtain rod or on a mounting board inside or outside the window frame. Mounting boards are cut from 1" (2.5 cm) lumber; the depth may be 2" to 5" (5 to 12.5 cm), or more, depending on the return of the underdrapery, curtain, or shade. Valances are generally "soft," as opposed to a "hard" cornice constructed of plywood.

Pouf valances are variations of soft cloud or balloon shades, made by shirring fabric on two curtain rods. The *double pouf* valance uses three curtain rods. For deeper headings and taller windows, Continental® rods may also be used for pouf valances.

Swags are soft drapes of fabric across the top of the window. They are usually attached to a mounting board, although a more informal look is to drape a swag over a wooden or decorative pole. They usually have an attached side drape of fabric, called either a *jabot* or a *cascade*. Jabots may be pleated, gathered, or casually draped.

Cornices are custom-built boxes without backs that cover the top of the window. They may be stained, painted, or upholstered to match a window treatment. The lower edge of a cornice may be cut straight or cut into a decorative shape.

Measuring for a Top Treatment

For mounting a top treatment over draperies, add 4" (10 cm) to the width, and 2" (5 cm) to the depth on each side, to allow for clearance at the return.

For scalloped treatments such as the Austrian or cloud valance, the shortest point of the scallop should come 4" (10 cm) below the top of the window glass and cover 6" to 8" (15 to 20.5 cm) of an undrapery heading.

If a valance or cornice is not mounted at the ceiling, allow at least 4" (10 cm) of clearance between the top of the drapery and the valance for the mounting brackets.

The top treatment should project at least 2" (5 cm) beyond the underdrapery for clearance. For example, if using a valance with one underdrapery, use a 5½" (14 cm) valance return over a standard 3½" (9 cm) underdrapery return.

Pouf Valance

The pouf valance is shirred on two curtain rods to create a soft, gathered top treatment. It can be casual and relaxed in mediumweight prints, but creates an elegant look in a sheer fabric, especially when used over sheer curtains and draperies. This valance can also be mounted on two tension rods for use as a shower curtain valance.

If the valance is installed over draperies, the projection on the curtain rods should clear the draperies by at least 2" (5 cm). To make the valance stand away from the drapery, use rods that have at least 1" (2.5 cm) difference in the return. The deeper return may be used as the lower rod to clear a drapery, or the shorter return may be used as the lower rod to allow the fabric to pouf with a more natural flare.

Mount the lower rod up to half the length of the valance. For example, for a 14" (35.5 cm) valance install the lower rod about 7" (18 cm) below the upper rod. You may prefer to mount the lower rod after the valance is finished because every fabric will pouf differently.

✄ Cutting Directions

Cut valance 2½ to 3 times the finished width, and 2 times the estimated length from top of upper rod to lowest point of valance to allow enough fabric for rod pockets, double heading, and pouffing.

YOU WILL NEED

Decorator fabric for valance.

Two flat curtain rods with 1" (2.5 cm) difference in returns. Continental® rod may be used for top rod.

How to Sew a Pouf Valance

1) Mount upper rod. To estimate length, drape a tape measure from the rod, down to the desired position, and back up to the lower rod position. (Lower rod has been mounted to show position.)

2) Seam widths of fabric together. Turn under and stitch double 1" (2.5 cm) side hems. Turn under ½" (1.3 cm), then allowance for rod pocket and heading. Stitch rod pocket and heading.

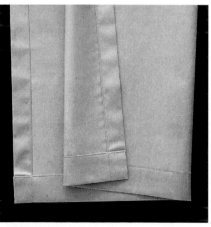

3) Turn under ½" (1.3 cm), then allowance for rod pocket on lower edge of valance; stitch. Insert curtain rods into rod pockets. Position and mount lower rod. Adjust poufs.

Double Pouf Valance

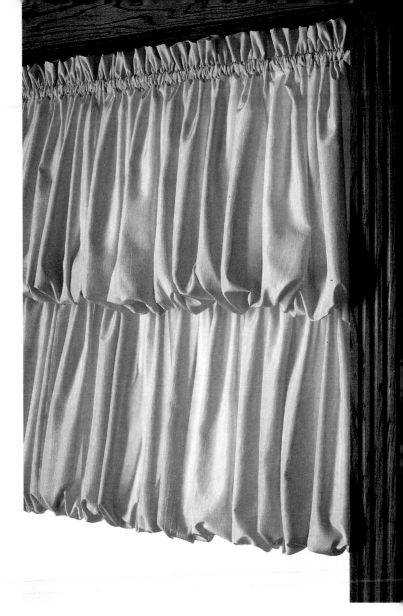

The double pouf is simply an extension of the pouf valance with an extra rod pocket stitched in the center. Three curtain rods are used for installation, with the middle rod mounted an equal distance from the upper and lower rods.

The double pouf can cover up to half the window. When used without an undercurtain, the valance can also be mounted on tension rods inside the window frame. Shutters or cafe curtains may be used on the lower half of the window.

The cut length does not have to be exact, because the fabric poufs and the distance between rods can be adjusted. If the fabric seems too limp and does not pouf as much as you would like, use lightly crumpled tissue paper in the poufs.

✂ Cutting Directions

Cut valance 2½ to 3 times the finished width, and 2 times the estimated length from top of upper rod to lowest point of valance to allow enough fabric for rod pockets, double heading, and pouffing.

YOU WILL NEED

Decorator fabric for valance.

Three flat curtain rods or tension rods.

How to Sew a Double Pouf Valance

1) Mount upper rod. Drape tape measure to estimate length of poufs and overall length of valance. (Lower and middle rods have been mounted to show position.)

2) Seam widths of fabric; stitch side hems, upper and lower rod pockets, and heading. Fold valance in half, right sides together; match upper and lower rod pockets. Stitch rod pocket 1½" (3.8 cm) from fold.

3) Insert curtain rods into rod pockets. Position and mount rods as desired. Adjust poufs.

Cloud Valance

The cloud valance is a short variation of the cloud shade, with gentle poufs or scallops across the bottom and a shirred heading at the top. It can be shirred on a flat curtain rod or Continental® rod, made with shirring tape and attached with hooks through the shirring tape to a curtain rod, or attached to a mounting board.

The first thing to determine is the number of scallops. They are usually 9" to 15" (23 to 38 cm) apart. Measure the width of the curtain rod or mounting board, and divide by the desired number of scallops. If the resulting number is greater than 15" (38 cm), add another scallop and divide again. This figure is the finished width of each scallop.

Determine the finished length at the shortest point (see Measuring for a Top Treatment, page 53). Remember that the scallop will fall below this point.

For a ruffled cloud valance, include the finished length of the ruffle in the measurement.

✂ Cutting Directions

Cut fabric 2 to 3 times the width of the rod. To finished length, add 12" (30.5 cm) for pouffing at lower edge; add allowance for double heading and rod pocket, plus ½" (1.3 cm) to turn under.

YOU WILL NEED

Decorator fabric for valance.

Shade tape or ring tape, total length equal to number of poufs, plus one, times cut length of valance.

Flat curtain rod or Continental® rod.

Wooden dowel for weight rod, the finished width of valance.

How to Sew a Cloud Valance

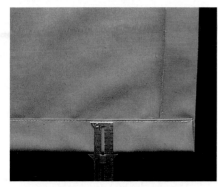

1) Seam fabric if necessary for width. Turn under and press 1" (2.5 cm) side hems; stitch double 1" (2.5 cm) bottom hem.

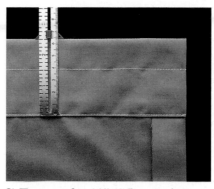

2) Turn under ½" (1.3 cm), then amount for rod pocket and heading. For 1½" (3.8 cm) rod pocket and 1" (2.5 cm) heading, turn under 2½" (6.5 cm). Stitch first fold, then 1½" (3.8 cm) away for rod pocket.

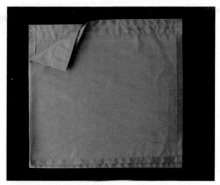

3) Divide width by number of scallops. For example, if hemmed width is 72" (183 cm), for three scallops the width of each scallop before shirring is 24" (61 cm). Mark at top and bottom of valance.

4) Cut shade or ring tape, and position at sides and at each marking, with folds of tape or rings even at top of hem. Stitch both sides of tape in same direction. Use zipper foot for ring tape.

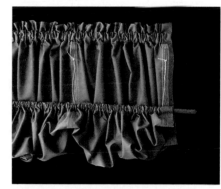

5) Pull up cords in shade or ring tape, and tie cords together in square knot to create pouf at the bottom of the valance.

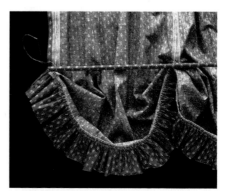

6) Cover wooden dowel with matching fabric for weight rod. Insert dowel into bottom hem. A weight rod is not necessary, but the valance may hang better; without it the pouf is looser.

How to Sew a Ruffled Cloud Valance

1) Cut ruffle 2 times the lower edge of valance and double the finished ruffle width plus 1" (2.5 cm). Fold in half lengthwise. Finish ends with narrow hem. To gather, zigzag over cord, or use ruffler attachment or shirring foot.

2) Press under 1" (2.5 cm) side hems of valance. Stitch ruffle on right side of valance in ½" (1.3 cm) seam, folding side hem to front over the ruffle. Zigzag or serge seam.

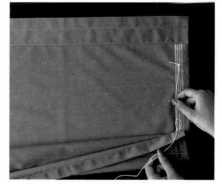

3) Follow steps 2 to 5, above, to finish ruffled cloud valance. Hand-tack covered dowel at each scallop. Ruffle falls gracefully into position at lower edge of valance.

Austrian Valance

The Austrian valance is a shortened version of the elegant Austrian shade, characterized by vertical rows of shirring, horizontal gathers, and soft scallops at the lower edge. Sheer and soft fabrics work best for this treatment, which is often trimmed with fringe. The valance is unlined to gather and drape beautifully.

There can be any number of scallops across the lower edge, but they are usually about 8" to 12" (20.5 to 30.5 cm) apart. This measurement may vary for wider or narrower windows. To determine the finished width of each scallop, divide the width of the mounting board by the number of scallops desired.

For an outside mount, cover the mounting board with matching fabric. The valance may also be mounted inside the window frame.

✄ Cutting Directions
Cut fabric 1½ times the width of mounting board and 2½ times the finished length. Cut sheer fabric 3 times the length. If it is necessary to seam widths together, position seams at shirring lines.

YOU WILL NEED

Decorator fabric for valance and, if desired, for mounting board.

Two-cord shirring tape, the cut length of valance (plus extra for finishing) times number of scallops, plus one.

1" (2.5 cm) twill tape, width of finished valance plus 1" (2.5 cm).

Optional trim, the cut width of the valance, plus extra for finishing.

Mounting board, 1" × 2" (2.5 × 5 cm), heavy-duty stapler, staples; tacks or pushpins.

Two angle irons for mounting.

Wooden dowel for weight rod, the finished width of valance.

How to Sew an Austrian Valance

1) Seam fabric if necessary for width. Press under 1½" (3.8 cm) on each side. For trim at lower edge, press ½" (1.3 cm) at bottom of curtain to *right* side. Pin heading of trim over raw edge; stitch. For valance without trim, stitch double 1" (2.5 cm) hem.

2) Divide cut width by number of scallops. For example, if the hemmed width is 72" (183 cm) and there are four scallops, the width of each scallop before shirring is 18" (46 cm). Mark at upper and lower edges.

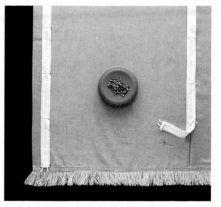

3) Pin 2-cord shirring tape from lower to upper edge on each mark. Place tape 1" (2.5 cm) from sides to cover raw edges. Stitch both edges of tape in same direction.

4) Tie cords at bottom so they will not pull out; pull shirring tape cords from top, gathering all cords to the same finished length. Secure ends of cord with knot.

5) Mark mounting board to match *finished* width of scallops. Valance is wider than mounting board. Match tape to marks, and tack. Divide excess fabric evenly on each side of markings; pleat and pin in place.

6) Remove valance from mounting board. Stitch twill tape over raw edge to finish upper edge and to use for mounting.

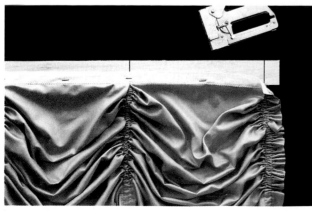

7) Staple or tack twill tape to top of mounting board. Place staples 6" (15 cm) apart.

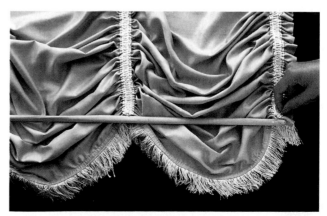

8) Cover wooden dowel with matching fabric. Hand-tack to back of valance at shirring lines.

Tapered Valance

The graceful curve of a tapered valance frames a window in soft folds of fabric. This valance is often used over mini-blinds and pleated shades to soften severe lines, or with short cafe curtains for a comfortable, casual look.

Tapered valances are usually lined when print fabrics are used, because you see the wrong side of the fabric as it cascades down the side of the window. If the lower edge has a ruffled finish, however, it does not have to be lined because the fall of the ruffle hides the wrong side of the fabric. Lightweight or sheer fabrics are also good choices for a ruffled valance, and do not require a lining.

The side length can be to the sill or apron, but it should be no less than one-third the length of the window. To check the curve, you may wish to make a paper pattern or mock-up with old sheets or lining fabric.

✄ Cutting Directions

Cut fabric and lining 2 times the width of the rod. To estimate length, measure at longest point and add amount for rod pocket and heading plus 1" (2.5 cm) for seam allowance and turn-under. For unlined valance with ruffle, use 2½ times fullness for valance. Subtract width of ruffle from finished length. Cut ruffle 2 times the length of the curve and finished width plus 1" (2.5 cm); seam fabric as necessary. Measure the curve after cutting the valance; or make a test muslin, and measure.

YOU WILL NEED

Decorator fabric for valance.

Lining for valance.

Flat curtain rod or Continental® rod.

How to Sew a Tapered Valance

1) Seam fabric widths as necessary. Divide and mark fabric vertically into thirds. Fold in half. At center, mark finished length plus ½" (1.3 cm). At side, mark depth of return. Draw a straight line from return mark to nearest one-third marking at finished length in center.

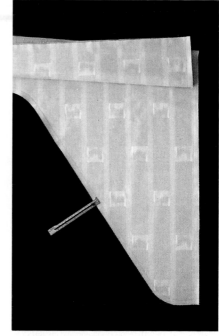

2) Round upper corner into gentle curve; repeat for lower corner at return. Pin fabric layers together, and cut both layers as one. Center third is straight. Cut lining, using valance as pattern.

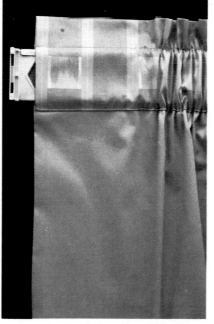

3) Place right side of lining and valance fabric together. Stitch ½" (1.3 cm) seam around valance, leaving upper edge open.

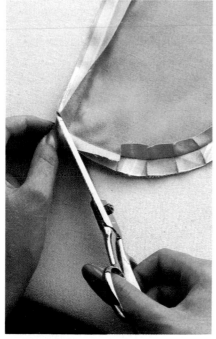

4) Press lining seam allowance toward lining. Clip curve. Diagonally trim corners.

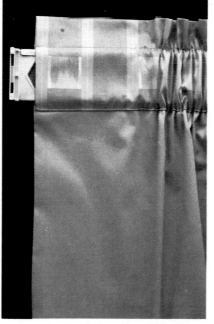

5) Turn right side out. Turn under and stitch rod pocket and heading. Insert curtain rod in pocket.

Unlined valance with ruffle. Stitch 1" (2.5 cm) double side hems on valance. Turn under and stitch rod pocket and heading. Make and attach ruffle as on page 107.

Swags & Jabots

A classic *swag* is a draping of soft folds used as a top treatment with pleated or gathered side panels. The side panels of the treatment are the *jabots* or *cascades*.

Window width and personal preference determine the number of swags. Each swag should generally be no wider than 40" (102 cm). This size can be adapted to any window size by increasing or decreasing the overlap on adjoining swags, as shown on page 52. The length of a swag is usually from 15" to 20" (38 to 51 cm) at the longest point in the center. Shallower swags may be used on narrow windows.

The jabot length should be about one-third of the drapery or window length, or should fall to a point of interest, such as the sill or floor. Its shortest point should be lower than the center of the swag. Jabots are 9" to 11" (23 to 28 cm) wide. Pleated jabots are more formal than gathered jabots, which are less controlled. Instructions are given here for the pleated jabot, but cutting and sewing techniques are basically the same for a gathered jabot. To gather the jabot, zigzag over a cord and pull the cord up to the desired fullness.

For outside mounting, attach swags and jabots to a cornice or mounting board placed 4" (10 cm) above the molding if used alone, or about 4" (10 cm) above the drapery rod if they are used over draperies. The cornice return must be deep enough to clear the underdrapery. Jabot returns are the same width as the cornice or mounting board. In homes with beautiful moldings the swags may be mounted inside the window on a board that fits inside the frame, and there are no returns.

Make a test swag to use as a pattern for cutting the decorator fabric. Use muslin or an old sheet that will drape softly. The test swag provides an opportunity to experiment and determine the appearance you want. Do not hesitate to drape the muslin and pin it at different positions until you find the look you like.

For each jabot, you will need one width of decorator fabric and lining the length of the jabot plus 1" (2.5 cm). For each swag, you will need 1 yd. (.95 m) of decorator fabric and lining if draped tape measurement, left, is less than the fabric width; you will need 2 yd. (1.85 m) if draped measurement is more than the fabric width.

YOU WILL NEED

Muslin or an old sheet for test swag.

Decorator fabric and lining for swags and jabots.

Wide twill tape, width of the mounting board plus 2 times the return.

Mounting board or cornice; heavy-duty stapler.

How to Estimate the Size of a Swag

Drape a tape measure or string to simulate the planned shape of each swag. For double swags, drape two tape measures.

How to Cut Jabots and Swags

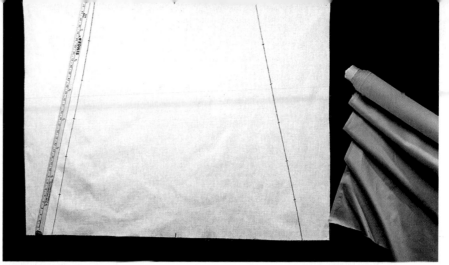

Jabots. Cut jabot 3 times finished width plus return and 1" (2.5 cm) seam allowance. On one side, mark shortest point plus 1" (2.5 cm). On the other side, mark longest point plus 1" (2.5 cm). From longest point, measure the width of return plus ½" (1.3 cm). Connect marks.

Swag. Cut muslin for the test swag 36" (91.5 cm) long. Cut the width the measurement from draped tape measure (left) plus 2" (5 cm) on each side for final adjustments. Mark width of window, centering marks at top of fabric. At lower edge, mark width from tape measure; connect the marks, forming diagonal guidelines. Divide each guideline equally into one more space than the number of folds; mark. For example, for five folds, divide into six spaces.

How to Make a Test Swag for Pattern

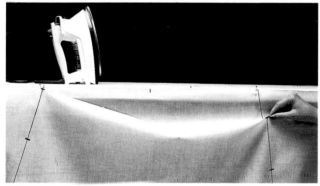

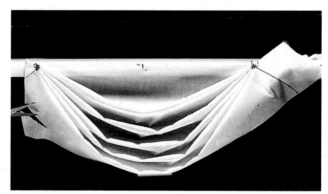

1) Fold muslin on first mark of diagonal line, and pull fold to the mark for upper corner; pin to ironing board. Continue pinning marked folds to corners, alternating sides and keeping upper edge straight.

2) Check the drape, and adjust pins and pleats as necessary. When folds are adjusted as desired, trim excess fabric 1" (2.5 cm) from outer edges and along the curved bottom edge about 3" (7.5 cm) from last fold.

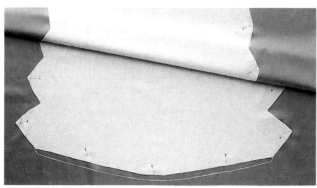

3) Unpin folds. Fold in half lengthwise to check that it is balanced and even; adjust cutting lines. Use as a pattern for cutting swag and lining. Add ½" (1.3 cm) seam allowances on upper and lower edges. This swag is not finished on ends and is mounted under jabot.

Alternative style. Fold muslin at first marks, and bring fold up to mounting board about 5" (12.5 cm) from ends. Drape smoothly, and continue folding, pulling each fold up and out slightly, toward end of board. The swag is finished at ends and can be mounted on top of or under jabot.

1) Pin lining to swag, right sides together, along lower curved edge. Stitch curved edge in ½" (1.3 cm) seam. Press lining seam allowance toward lining. Turn right side out; press stitched edge.

2) Pin swag front and lining together at remaining three sides. Overlock or zigzag raw edges together.

3) Pin pleats in place. The outside edge of each notch is the fold point.

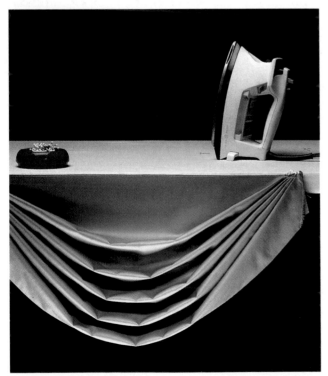

4) Check drape of swag again by pinning swag to the side of ironing board or mounting board. Make minor adjustments as desired.

5) Stitch across all folds to hold pleats in place.

How to Sew Jabots

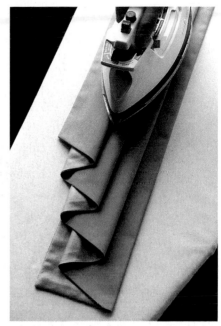

1) Place jabot lining and fabric, right sides together; stitch ½" (1.3 cm) seam on sides and bottom. Press lining seam allowance toward lining. Clip corners, and turn right side out. Press stitched edges. Stitch upper edges together in ½" (1.3 cm) seam. Zigzag or overlock raw edges.

2) Lay jabot, wrong side up, on large flat surface. On sides, fold under return and press in place. Turn jabot right side up.

3) Fold into evenly spaced pleats, starting on the outer edge; steam in position. Pleat other jabot in opposite direction. Check pleats by hanging jabot over edge of ironing board. Stitch ⅜" (1 cm) from upper edge to hold pleats in place.

How to Attach Swag and Jabots to a Mounting Board

1) Center swag on mounting board or cornice with edge of swag ½" (1.3 cm) from edge of board. Staple swag to board at 6" (15 cm) intervals.

2) Place top of one jabot at end of mounting board, with pressed fold at corner. Staple return in place. Position pleats on mounting board, overlapping swag. Fold under excess fabric at corner, and staple.

3) Cover fabric edges with wide twill tape. Staple tape along both edges, mitering at corners.

Padded Cornices

A cornice is a painted or fabric-covered wooden frame used as a tailored top treatment. When fabric-covered, the frame is padded with foam or bonded polyester to round the corners and give it a soft, upholstered look.

A cornice not only frames and finishes a window treatment by hiding the hardware, but also provides good insulation and energy-saving efficiency, because it encloses the top of the treatment and prevents cold air from escaping into the room.

Cornices are usually custom-built to fit the window. With simple carpentry skills you can build a cornice from plywood or pine boards. Any imperfections in the carpentry are covered with padding and fabric.

Measure the outside frame of the window after the drapery hardware is in place. The cornice should clear the curtain or drapery heading by at least 3" (7.5 cm), and it should extend at least 2" (5 cm) beyond the end of the drapery on each side. The measurements are the cornice *inside* measurements. Allow for the thickness of the wood when cutting.

The cornice should completely cover the drapery headings and hardware. Generally, apply the same guidelines for height as for any other top treatment. The cornice should be about one-fifth the height of the window treatment.

Use contrasting welting around the top and bottom edges to set the cornice apart when it is covered with the same fabric as the drapery.

When estimating fabric, railroad the fabric on a cornice to eliminate seams on plain fabrics. If the fabric cannot be railroaded because of a directional print, place the seams inconspicuously, never in the center. Prints should be centered or balanced.

✂ Cutting Directions

For face piece, cut decorator fabric 6" (15 cm) wider than front plus sides, and the height of cornice plus 3" (7.5 cm). Cut a 4" (10 cm) inner lining strip from decorator fabric, the same width as the face piece. Cut a strip of lining fabric the same width as the face piece and the same height as the cornice.

Cut a strip of batting or foam to cover the front and sides of the cornice.

Cover cording, page 111, step 1, to make welting slightly longer than the distance around the lower edge.

YOU WILL NEED

Decorator fabric and lining to cover cornice; optional coordinating or contrasting fabric for welting.

To build the cornice, ½" (1.3 cm) plywood for the front, top, and sides; carpenter's glue; sixpenny finishing nails.

To pad the cornice, 1" (2.5 cm) bonded polyester upholstery batting or ½" (1.3 cm) foam. If not available in local stores, you may be able to obtain through an upholsterer or upholstery supply.

5/32" cording slightly longer than the distance to be corded.

Cardboard upholsterer's stripping to cover lower edge and sides; heavy-duty stapler, ½" (1.3 cm) and ¼" (6 mm) staples; spray foam adhesive; angle irons for mounting.

How to Build a Cornice

1) **Measure** and cut top to correspond to inside measurements for clearance. Cut front same width as top, and desired height. Cut sides same height as cornice and depth of top piece plus thickness of plywood.

2) **Glue** the top in place to front of board first. Remember which edges abut. Nail to secure. Then attach sides, first gluing in place to hold and then securing with nails.

How to Pad and Cover a Cornice

1) Stitch welting on right side of face piece in ½" (1.3 cm) seam, raw edges even. Sew welted edge to inner lining strip; sew free edge of inner strip to lining. Fold face piece in half to mark center at top and bottom.

2) Mark center of cornice at top and bottom. Place *wrong* side of face fabric on outside of cornice, with welting seam on front edge of cornice; match center markings. Tack.

5) Fold lining to inside. Fold under raw edge, and staple at inside where top and face meet; at lower corners, miter fabric and staple close to corner. Tuck excess fabric into upper corners, and staple.

6) Rip excess welting seam back to end of cornice; trim welting to 1" (2.5 cm). Trim cord even with cornice edge. Staple lining to wall end of cornice; trim excess lining. Staple welting to wall end.

9) Tack at center and ends, removing slack. Do not stretch too tightly. Starting at center, turn under raw edge and staple to each end, placing staples 1½" (3.8 cm) apart, smoothing fabric as you go.

10) Pull fabric around corner to top back corner, removing slack; tack. Fold side fabric to back edge; staple. Trim excess fabric at back edge.

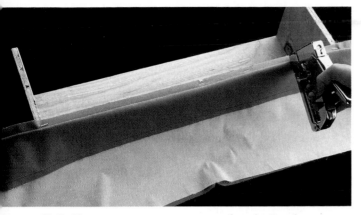

3) **Pull** seam taut to corners, and tack. Staple every 4" (10 cm) from center to ends. Flip lining back to check that welting is straight.

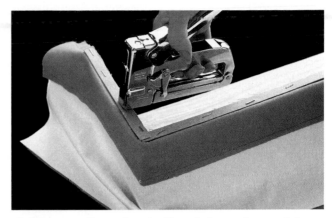

4) **Place** cardboard stripping tight against welting seam. Staple every 1" to 1½" (2.5 to 3.8 cm). Cut and overlap stripping at corners.

7) **Turn** cornice face up. Apply adhesive to front and sides. Place padding over glued surface, and stretch it slightly toward each end. Allow glue to set.

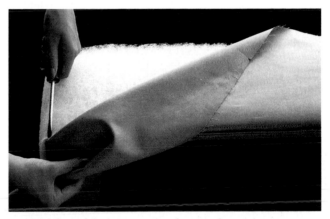

8) **Fold** face fabric over the front of cornice. Use a screwdriver to hold padding in place at corners. Gently smooth fabric toward top of cornice.

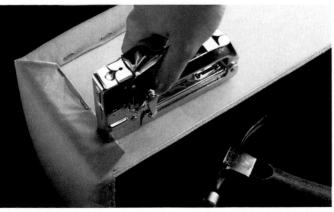

11) **Fold** fabric diagonally at corner to form a miter. Staple at corner and across ends. If fabric is bulky, tap staple with hammer. Repeat on both corners.

Welting at upper edge. Staple welting to sides and front, with seam at edge. On cornice front, place fabric over welting, with right sides together and raw edges even. Staple cardboard stripping at front and side edges as in step 4, above. Pull fabric to top of cornice, and fold under at sides and back; staple next to folds.

Bed & Bath

Sewing for the Bedroom & Bath

The bedroom and bath are often thought of together because of the fabric and color coordination. It is also a good area to try your hand at sewing projects because the typical fabrics for these rooms are easy to work with. Although a spread, comforter, or shower curtain may be bulky to handle, there are few measurements to take and the straight seaming and hems are simple to sew.

Start with a shower curtain and a coordinated valance. A sink skirt and embellished towels complete the look. Consider sewing a duvet cover for a comforter, with a coordinated dust skirt and shams. Shirring on upper and lower edges gives a custom look to the dust skirt. The same technique can be used, on a smaller scale, as a border on the pillow sham. As a finishing touch, upholster a headboard in fabric. For a daybed, a tailored cover with a dust ruffle is a practical covering if the daybed is used for lounging.

Measuring the Bed

Measure the bed with the blankets and sheets that are normally on the bed. This may make the measurements larger than the actual mattress size, but it will ensure that the bedcover is not skimpy and that fitted covers fit the bed perfectly.

Measure from side to side across the top of the mattress for width, and from the head to the foot of the bed for length.

Comforters, coverlets, and duvets reach 3" to 4" (7.5 to 10 cm) below the mattress on two sides and at the foot of the bed. The drop length is the distance from the upper edge of the mattress to the bottom of the comforter, usually 9" to 12" (23 to 30.5 cm), depending on the depth of the mattress.

For dust skirt length, measure from the top of the bed frame for daybeds, or the top of the box spring for regular beds, to the floor.

To determine how many widths of fabric are needed, divide the total width of the bedcover by the fabric width; round off to the next highest number. Most bedcovers require two or three fabric widths. Multiply the number of widths by the length of the bedcover for amount of fabric needed. Divide by 36" (100 cm) to determine the number of yards (meters).

For most bedcovers you will need to seam the panels together. Cut one full width for the center and two equal, partial-width panels for each side. If the fabric has a large print motif, be sure to allow extra fabric for matching at seams.

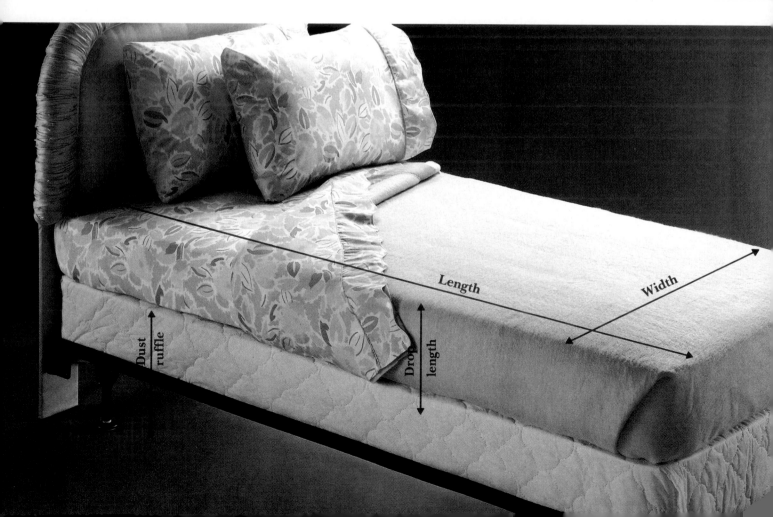

Length

Width

Dust ruffle

Drop length

Sewing with Sheets

Sheets are practical for duvet covers because their width makes seaming and matching unnecessary, but they are not always printed on-grain, and the design does not match at the selvage as with decorator fabrics. If all four sides of the sheet are hemmed, the sheet may have been cut on the crosswise, instead of lengthwise, grain. Consider the grainline before tearing or cutting sheets.

The sizes given below are general guidelines to use in determining how many sheets will be needed for the duvet or comforter cover. Comforters and sheets may vary in size, especially after laundering. Preshrink all-cotton sheets and flannel sheets before cutting.

Except for a crib-size cover, which can be made from one twin-size sheet, you will need two appropriately sized sheets for the comforter or duvet cover. There will be enough fabric left on the sides of the two sheets to cut piping strips. Use an extra flat sheet to trim the duvet with a self-ruffle.

Sheet Requirements for Duvet Covers

Bed Size	Sheets for Duvet Cover	Sheets for 4" (10 cm) Self-Ruffle	Number of 1½" (3.2 cm) Piping Strips	Standard Duvet Sizes
Crib	1 twin flat	1 twin flat	3 lengthwise strips	42" × 52" (107 × 132 cm)
Bunk	2 twin flat	1 twin flat	5 lengthwise strips	59" × 82" (150 × 208 cm)
Twin	2 twin flat	1 twin flat	5 lengthwise strips	68" × 86" (73 × 218 cm)
Full	2 full flat	1 twin flat	5 lengthwise strips	76" × 86" (195 × 218 cm)
Queen	2 queen flat	1 full flat	5 lengthwise strips	86" × 86" (218 × 218 cm)
King	2 king flat	1 full flat	4 lengthwise strips	101" × 86" (257 × 218 cm)

Squaring Corners of Sheets

Determine direction of grain. To determine lengthwise grain, hold a section of sheet and pull in both directions. The direction with the least amount of stretch is the lengthwise grain.

Tear on lengthwise grain only. Measure from selvage, and tear along *lengthwise* grain for width. If you tear on crosswise grain, you will not get squared right angles.

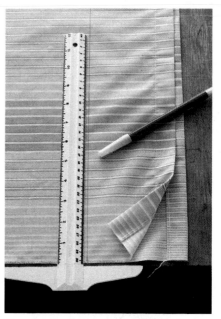

Cut on crosswise grain. Fold sheet in half lengthwise so it lies smooth with no twist; line up edges of fabric with table edge. Use a T-square to mark length. Cut with rotary cutter or shears.

Duvet Covers

A *duvet* is a plump comforter or continental quilt, puffed with down or fiberfill. To change the look of an existing comforter or to protect a muslin-colored duvet, sew a duvet cover. This cover is similar to a large pillowcase with a hidden zipper in the back so the cover can be easily removed for laundering.

Duvet covers are easier to sew than full-size bedspreads because they do not require as much fabric and are therefore not as bulky to handle. Sheets are an ideal fabric choice because they do not require seaming for full widths, and when used on the bed they do not require an additional top sheet. Even if you are not using sheets for the entire cover, you can use a sheet for the back of the duvet.

These covers also lend themselves to the use of decorative touches such as a ruffle on all edges, contrasting welting in the seam, or both. Tucks, applied decorative stripes, lace, or an appliqué may be stitched on the top.

✂ Cutting Directions

Measure the down or fiberfill duvet. For a snug fit, make the finished duvet cover 2" (5 cm) shorter and 2" (5 cm) narrower than duvet measurements.

Cut front 1" (2.5 cm) wider and 1" (2.5 cm) longer than finished size; cut the back the same width and 1½" (3.8 cm) shorter than the front. Cut zipper strip 3½" (9 cm) wide and the same length as the cut width of the back.

For welting, cut fabric strips 1½" (3.8 cm) wide and 2 times the length and 2 times the width of the duvet, plus a few inches extra for finishing. Cut 5/32" cording the same length as fabric strips.

For a 4" (10 cm) self-ruffle, cut fabric strips 9" (23 cm) wide. Join as necessary to get a strip that is 4 times the length plus 4 times the width of the duvet. For an eyelet ruffle, cut 4" to 6" (10 to 15 cm) eyelet edging 4 times the length plus 4 times the width. For pregathered eyelet trim, cut trim 2 times the length plus 2 times the width.

YOU WILL NEED

Flat sheets or washable cotton or cotton/polyester fabric for front and back. If using sheets, see page 73 for number of sheets needed. For fabric, measure bed and determine amount needed as on page 72.

Two zippers, 22" (56 cm) long.

Optional 5/32" cording, ruffling, or self-ruffling.

How to Sew a Duvet Cover with Welting

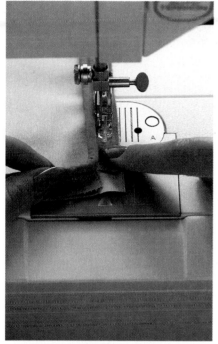

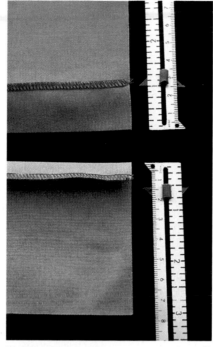

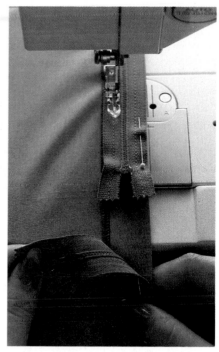

1) Make welting as in step 1, page 111. Stitch to right side of front in ⅜" (1 cm) seam. Clip and ease welting at corners. Join ends as in steps 3 to 5, page 111.

2) Overlock or zigzag upper edge of zipper strip and lower edge of the back. Press the finished edge of zipper strip under ½" (1.3 cm), and the finished edge of back under 1" (2.5 cm).

3) Place closed zippers face down on seam allowance of back, with tabs meeting in center and edge of zipper tapes on fold. Using zipper foot, stitch one side of zippers.

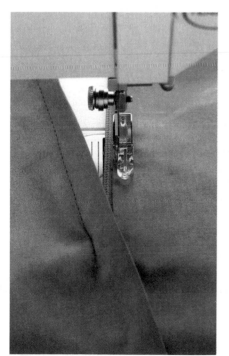

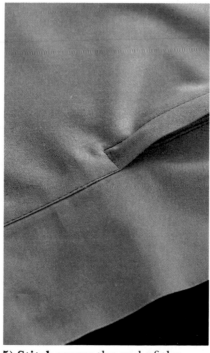

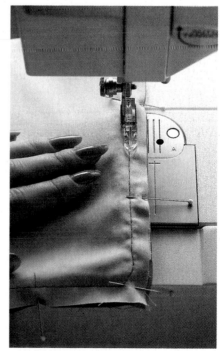

4) Turn right side up; place pressed edge of zipper strip along edge of teeth on other side of zippers, and stitch close to edge. Backstitch at end of zippers.

5) Stitch across the end of the zippers; then topstitch through all layers to close the seam from the end of the zippers to the side edges. Open the zippers.

6) Pin duvet front to back, right sides together. With front side up, stitch, using zipper foot; crowd stitches close to first stitching. Turn duvet cover right side out, and insert duvet.

How to Sew a Ruffled Duvet Cover

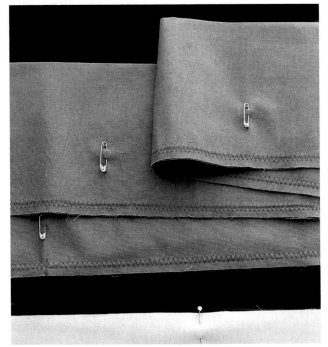

1) Join ends of ruffling strips to form circle. Fold in half lengthwise, right side out. Zigzag raw edges together ¼" (6 mm) from edge, using longest and widest stitch. Divide into four equal sections, and mark with safety pins; also mark center of each side of front.

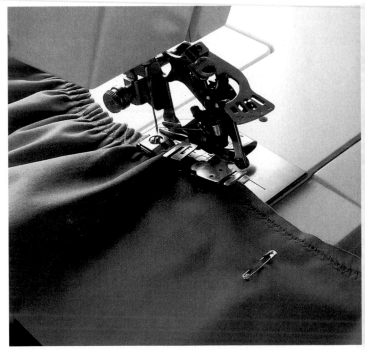

2) Use ruffler attachment or shirring foot, set for double fullness, to gather ruffle ⅜" (1 cm) from edge. Test on a scrap. It is easier to ruffle a little less than 2 to 1 and ease in gathers than to ruffle more tightly and have to clip threads, which may result in flat sections between gathers.

How to Sew a Duvet Cover with Ruffle and Welting

1) Follow steps 1 to 5 for cover with welting (page 75) and steps 1 and 2, opposite, for ruffled cover.

2) Pin and machine-baste ruffle to front over welting. Match ruffle to front, and ease in fullness as in step 3, below. Finish as in step 5, below; stitch, crowding welt.

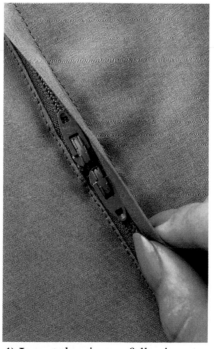

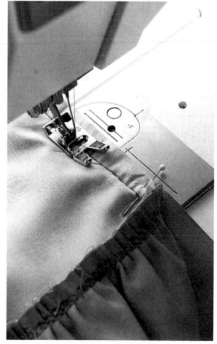

3) Match safety pins on ruffle to marks on front section. Pin and machine-baste ruffle to front, stitching just inside gathering row. Ease some extra fullness into ruffle at corners, so ruffle lies flat when turned to right side.

4) Insert the zipper, following steps 2 to 5 for cover with welting, page 75.

5) Pin front to back, right sides together. With front side up, stitch ½" (1.3 cm) from edges. Turn cover right side out, and insert duvet.

Tuck-pleated Dust Skirt

A fitted lining holds the tuck-pleated dust skirt in place. Although the skirt gives an upholstered look, the four corners are split to fit over the bed frame, then held together with short strips of hook and loop tape. The tape is attached to grosgrain ribbon that is sewn into the seam.

✂ Cutting Directions

If using a sheet or a fabric that lends itself to tearing, tear along the lengthwise grain to obtain strips the desired drop plus 1" (2.5 cm) for seam allowances; join strips together to make one strip 2 times the width and 4 times the length of bed, plus 40" (102 cm) for extensions at head of the bed.

For deck, cut flat sheet 1" (2.5 cm) wider and 1" (2.5 cm) longer than box spring.

Cut lining the same drop as the skirt; cut two pieces the length of box spring plus 1" (2.5 cm), and one piece the width of box spring plus 1" (2.5 cm); cut two extensions to wrap around the head of the bed 11" (28 cm) long.

Cut welting strips 1½" (3.8 cm) wide, and 2 times the length plus 2 times the width of the deck. Cut ⁵⁄₃₂" cording the same length as welting strips.

Cut 8 pieces of grosgrain and 8 pieces of hook and loop tape 2" (5 cm) long.

YOU WILL NEED

Decorator fabric or sheet for dust skirt on three sides of bed plus extensions.

Flat sheets for deck and lining.

Grosgrain ribbon, 1½" (3.8 cm) wide.

Hook and loop tape.

⁵⁄₃₂" cording for welting.

How to Sew a Tuck-pleated Dust Skirt

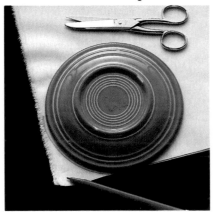

1) Fold deck in half lengthwise, then crosswise so all four cut or torn corners are together. Using a saucer for a guide, cut through all layers to curve corners gently.

2) Fold curved corners in half to determine centers; mark fold with ¼" (6 mm) clip through all layers.

3) Tuck-pleat skirt ⅜" (1 cm) from upper and lower edges, using ruffler attachment set at 2 to 1 fullness; keep right side of fabric up.

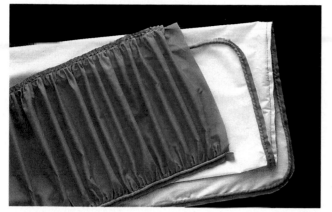

4) Make welting, page 111, step 1; machine-baste welting ⅜" (1 cm) from lower edge of pleated skirt and around deck edge. Steam press lightly to flatten tucks.

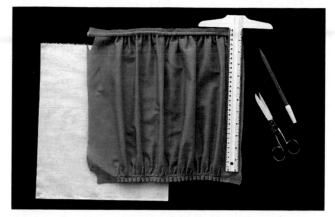

5) Cut lengths of pleated skirt to match lining pieces. Release a few pleats if necessary to flatten skirt for 1" (2.5 cm) at each end. Square and trim ends to match lining.

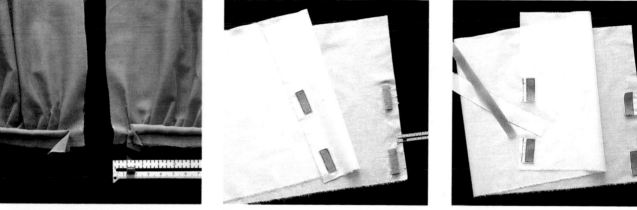

6) Cut ½" (1.3 cm) of cording out of ends of welting. Fold welting back on itself, and pin to square and finish ends.

7) Attach loop side of hook and loop tape to ends of long lining pieces; sew one strip ½" (1.3 cm) from raw edge and ½" (1.3 cm) from bottom, and second strip ½" (1.3 cm) from raw edge and in center of side.

8) Stitch hook side of hook and loop tape on grosgrain strips, ½" (1.3 cm) from edge. Stitch strips on remaining pieces of skirt, matching the tapes that were stitched in step 7.

9) Stitch lower and side edges of skirt to lining, right sides together. Turn skirt right side out, and machine-baste top edges of skirt to lining ⅜" (1 cm) from edge. Do not trim grosgrain ribbon.

10) Stitch upper edge of skirt sections to deck edges, right sides together. Skirt sections with tape extensions underlap adjacent section ¼" (6 mm) at corners. Serge or zigzag raw edges together.

How to Sew a Tuck-pleated Pillow Sham

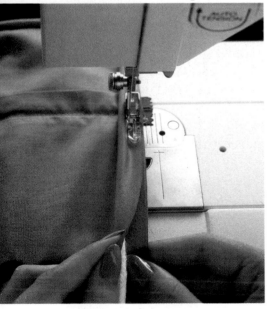

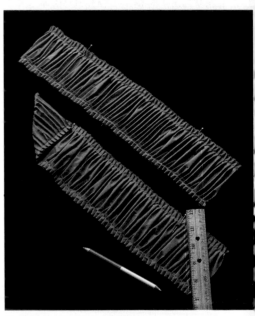

1) Insert zipper in back of sham, following instructions for zipper insertion in duvet, page 75, steps 2 to 5. Cover cording and machine-baste to right side of back in ⅜" (1 cm) seam; join ends of welting (page 111).

2) Tuck-pleat the border strip, ⅜" (1 cm) from both edges, using ruffler attachment at 2 to 1 ratio. Keep fabric same side up when pleating. Steam press finished strip lightly to flatten tucks.

3) Cut two strips 1" (2.5 cm) longer than finished sham length, and two strips 1" (2.5 cm) longer than finished sham width. On wrong side of short strips, fold corner back; mark width of strip with pin. Unfold; mark stitching angle from pin to corner.

Tuck-pleated Pillow Sham

The mitered, tuck-pleated border on this sham is a narrow version of the tuck-pleated dust skirt. The finished sham should be the same size as the pillow.

The technique for mitering a border around a pillow is also used for attaching a mitered stripe to a pillow or cushion (page 22).

✂ Cutting Directions

Cut the back 1" (2.5 cm) wider and 1½" (3.8 cm) shorter than the finished size. Cut a back zipper strip the same width as the back and 3½" (9 cm) wide. Cut the center of the front 4" (10 cm) narrower and shorter than finished sham; cut border strips 3½" (9 cm) wide and 4 times the length and width of the sham, plus extra for seaming strips.

For welting, cut strips 1½" (3.8 cm) wide and 2 times the length and 2 times the width of sham, plus extra for seaming.

YOU WILL NEED

Decorator fabric or sheets for sham.

Contrasting border fabric.

⁵⁄₃₂" **cording** for welting.

Zipper, 22" (56 cm) long.

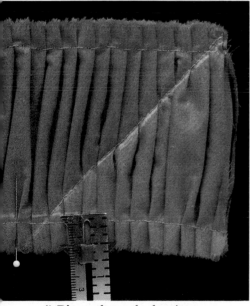

4) Pin each marked strip to an unmarked strip, and stitch from corner to ½" (1.3 cm) from raw edge; backstitch. Trim seams to ¼" (6 mm), and press open.

5) Pin inner edges of border to sham front; stitch one side at a time, backstitching (arrow) at both ends of seam.

6) Pin front to back, right sides together; stitch ½" (1.3 cm) from edge on all four sides. To finish, overlock or zigzag raw edges. Turn to right side; insert pillow.

Duvet Cover from Sheets

To use the decorative border on a sheet, conceal the zippered opening under the border on the right side of the cover. Or add a decorative border to a plain sheet, using lace or ribbon trims.

✂ Cutting Directions

Measure the down or fiberfill duvet. For snug fit, make the finished duvet cover 2" (5 cm) shorter and 2" (5 cm) narrower than duvet measurements.

For back of cover, cut or tear a sheet 1" (2.5 cm) wider and 1" (2.5 cm) longer than finished size.

For front, cut or tear bordered sheet 1" (2.5 cm) wider than finished size; for bordered zipper flap, right, fold sheet in half lengthwise and mark a line 20" (51 cm) from edge of sheet; for zipper strip, mark second line 3" (7.5 cm) from first line. Cut on both lines. To determine the length to cut the remaining front section, use chart at right. Line up sheet section with edge of table, and use a T-square to square lower edge.

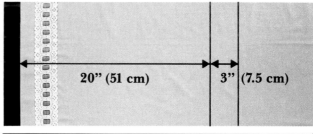

20" (51 cm)   3" (7.5 cm)

Cut Length of Duvet Cover Front	in. (cm)
1) Finished length of cover	
2) Bordered zipper flap, 20" (51 cm)	−
3) Width of border	+
4) 1" (2.5 cm) seam allowance	+
5) Front cut length	=

YOU WILL NEED

Flat sheets with decorative border. See page 73 for number and size of sheets.

Two zippers, 22" (56 cm) long.

How to a Sew a Duvet Cover from Sheets

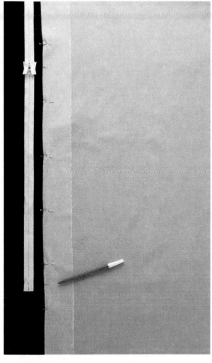

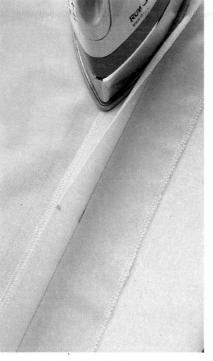

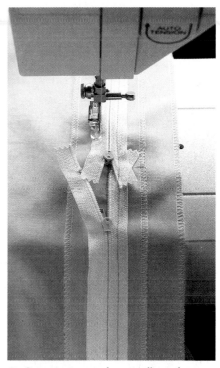

1) Zigzag or overedge raw edges of zipper strip and upper edge of front. Pin zipper strip to upper edge, right sides together. Mark zipper opening 22" (56 cm) in both directions from center.

2) Stitch 1"(2.5 cm) zipper seam, starting at one side. At zipper marking, backstitch, and then machine-baste across zipper opening; backstitch and continue to other edge. Press seam open.

3) Center open zippers face down on seam allowance, with teeth on basted seam and tab ends meeting in center. Using zipper foot, stitch on one side of teeth. Close zippers; stitch other side. Remove basting.

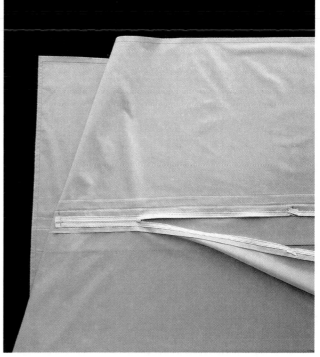

4) Pin decorative border section over zipper, right side up, with zipper seam 1" (2.5 cm) from inner edge of border. Stitch on edge of border through all layers. Open zippers.

5) Pin front to back, with right sides together and back side up. Stitch ½" (1.3 cm) from raw edge. To finish, serge or zigzag raw edges. Turn right side out; insert duvet.

How to Sew a Reverse Sham Bedcover

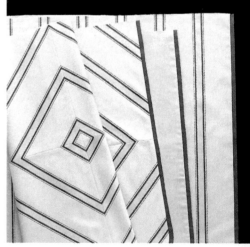

1) Fold face fabric and lining in half lengthwise. To round the corners at the foot of the cover and the top of the sham, line up corners evenly and use a saucer to mark curve. Cut on marked line.

2) Fold the bias strip in half lengthwise, wrong sides together; press. Stitch strip to curved sides on right side of cover and sham sections, stitching a scant ½" (1.3 cm) from edge. Ease strip around curves so it lies smooth when turned.

3) Pin lining to face fabric on both sections, right sides together in ½" (1.3 cm) seam; stitch around cover, leaving upper edge open. Trim corners, and turn both sections right side out.

Reverse Sham Bedcover

The reverse sham bedcover is an all-in-one cover for bed and pillows. It has an extra-deep flap at the top to fold back over the bed pillows, making the bed especially quick and easy to make.

The reverse sham technique can be adapted for duvets or full-size bedspreads. It also works as a sheet-weight bedcover for summer sleeping.

For a tailored feeling, without the look of separate pillow shams, add the sham extension to a duvet cover. Follow the instructions for a duvet cover (pages 74 to 77), leaving the upper edge open. Make the sham, and attach it as shown, below.

For versatility, use coordinating fabrics or sheets for the face and the lining and make the cover reversible. The edges are finished with a flat bias trim. If using a striped fabric, as shown here, the stripes may be mitered on the sham section for a decorative effect.

✂ Cutting Directions
Seam panels together as necessary for width. For the cover, cut the face fabric and lining the width of the

bed, plus 2 times the drop plus 1" (2.5 cm) seam allowance; cut the length the length of bed plus one drop, plus 1" (2.5 cm) for seam allowance.

For the sham, cut the face fabric and lining 28" (71 cm) deep and the same width as the cut width of the cover. This size is suitable for an average 20" (51 cm) pillow. For larger or smaller pillows, loosely measure over the curve of the pillow and add 1" (2.5 cm) for seam allowance. Cut sham in same direction as cover, matching stripes or motifs, unless stripes are mitered for decorative effect.

For trim, cut 2" (5 cm) bias strips of contrasting fabric 2 times the finished length plus 2 times the finished width, plus extra for seam allowances.

YOU WILL NEED

Decorator fabric and lining for bedcover.
Contrasting fabric for bias trim.

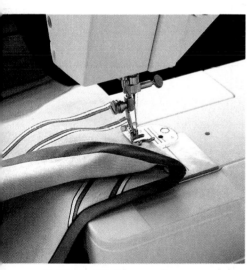

4) Bastestitch raw edges together across open ends of cover and sham. To stitch concealed French seam, match *wrong* side of sham to *right* side of cover. Stitch ¼" (6 mm) seam; press. Trim, turn, press, and stitch ⅜" (1 cm) from fold.

4a) Alternative seam. Match *right* side of sham to *wrong* side of cover, and stitch ½" (1.3 cm) seam; trim. Finish seam with zigzag or overlock stitch, or apply tricot bias binding.

5) Place cover on bed with pillows on top of cover. Fold reverse sham back over pillows. Seam is inside when sham is turned back.

Daybed Dust Skirt & Tufted Cover

This tailored daybed set combines a fitted, tufted cover with a gathered dust skirt. The daybed cover is shaped at the corners to fit smoothly around the frame of the bed.

Most daybed frames have rims on either two or four sides to keep the mattress from shifting; other frames have no rims. Make adjustments accordingly so the dust skirt hangs from the top of the frame or rim, is open at the corners, and hangs evenly ¼" (6 mm) from the floor. For some daybed frames, it may be necessary to attach the dust skirt 1½" to 2" (3.8 to 5 cm) from the corners of the deck, so the gathers will not bunch at the corners. The drop of the cover will overlap the skirt to conceal the frame at the corners.

✂ Cutting Directions (Cover)

Cut center panel 60" (150 cm) long from full width of fabric. Divide another width in half for the side panels; join side panels to center panel, matching design at seams. Trim excess fabric from each side panel so width measures 96" (244 cm).

Cut and seam lining 1" (2.5 cm) longer and 1" (2.5 cm) wider than top.

Cut strips of fabric for welting. Join ends to make a strip 9 yds. (8.25 m) long.

✂ Cutting Directions (Deck & Skirt)

Cut dust skirt deck the length and width of the frame plus 1" (2.5 cm) for seam allowances. For daybeds with rims, cut a strip of decorator fabric for each rim the height of the rim plus 1" (2.5 cm) for seam allowances, and the length or width of the frame plus 2" (5 cm) for hem allowances.

Cut two skirt sections each 2 times the length of the deck plus 2" (5 cm) for hems. Cut two skirt sections each 2 times the width of deck plus 2" (5 cm) for hem. To determine skirt length, measure as in step 1, opposite.

YOU WILL NEED

For dust skirt, 6¼ yd. (5.75 m) of 54" (140 cm) decorator fabric and one twin flat sheet for deck.

For cover top and lining, 3⅜ yd. (3.10 m) of 54" (140 cm) fabric, plus extra for matching and welting.

Extra lofty polyester batting, 60" × 96" (150 × 244 cm).

Cording, 9 yd. (8.25 m).

Narrow ribbon for ties, 18 yd. (17.5 m) of ⅛" (3 mm) ribbon; crewel needle; about 13 dozen safety pins.

How to Sew a Daybed Dust Skirt

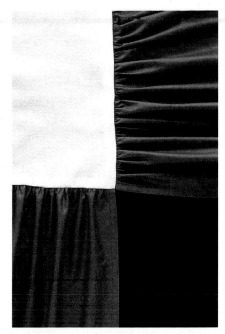

1) Measure frame to determine finished length **(a)** and width **(b)**. To determine skirt length, measure from frame **(c)** to floor and add 2½" (6.5 cm). For sides with rims, measure from top of rim **(d)** to floor and add 2½" (6.5 cm).

2) Press under and stitch double 1" (2.5 cm) hem on lower edge of each skirt section. Gather upper edge, using any method on page 106. For sides with rims, match skirt section to fabric strip, right sides together; stitch ½" (1.3 cm) seam. On all skirt sections, press under and stitch double ½" (1.3 cm) side hems.

3a) For bed without rims. Pin skirt sections to sides of deck, right sides together, with edges of ruffle meeting at each corner. Stitch ½" (1.3 cm) seam. Finish seams with zigzag or overlock stitch.

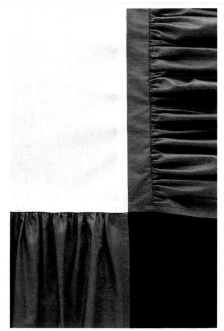

3b) For bed with two rims. For sides that do not have rims, attach to deck as in step 3a. For sides that have rims, stitch strips to edges of deck in ½" (1.3 cm) seam.

3c) For bed with four rims. Stitch strips to edges of deck, right sides together, in ½" (1.3 cm) seam; finish seams with zigzag or overlock stitch.

4) Place dust skirt over frame of daybed, adjusting ruffles so the deck seam is on the upper edge of rim or even with the edge of the frame. Replace mattress on frame.

How to Sew a Tufted Daybed Cover

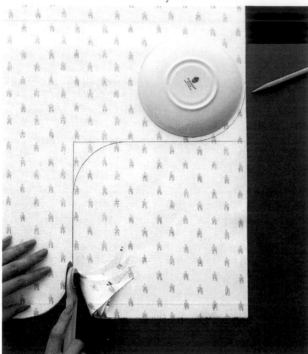

1) Fold top in half lengthwise, then crosswise, with right sides together and corners matching. Draw a 9½" (24 cm) square at matched corner. (This is the corner *without* any folds.) Using a saucer as a pattern, draw three curves as shown. Cut on curved line.

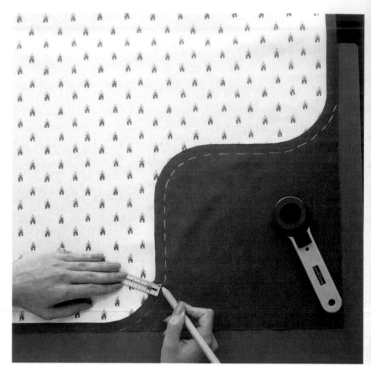

2) Place top over lining so ½" (1.3 cm) seam allowance extends beyond top at straight edges. Following curved corners on top, add ½" (1.3 cm) seam allowance and trim lining corners. Trim polyester batting to match lining.

5) Place lining, *wrong* side up, on large, flat surface. Place batting on lining; place top, *right* side up, on batting. Pin through all layers at each tufting location.

6) Thread needle with ribbon. At each tuft marker, insert needle from right side through all layers. Pull through bottom layer, leaving 4" (10 cm) tail at top for tying. Bring needle to the top ¼" (6 mm) away. Cut ribbon, leaving 4" (10 cm) tail; tie a square knot.

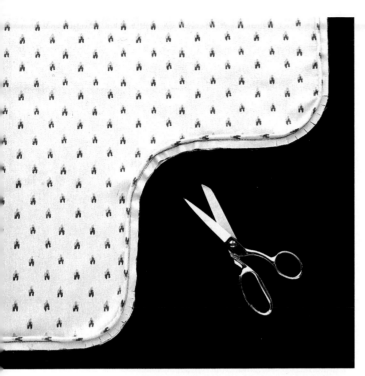

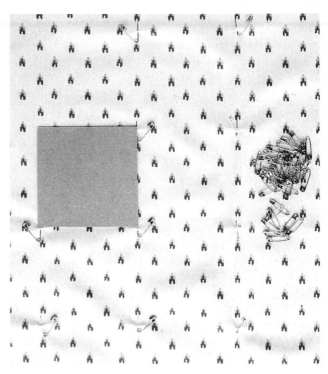

3) Cut and sew welting strips, page 111, step 1. Stitch welting to top in ½" (1.3 cm) seam, raw edges even. Clip seam allowances on inner curves; be careful not to stretch welting on outer curves.

4) Fold top in half lengthwise, then crosswise, to mark center. Mark tufting locations on right side of top, beginning at center and spacing tufts about 6" (15 cm) apart. Or use the fabric design to space tufts evenly.

7) Clip lining seam allowances on curves. Turn under ½" (1.3 cm) on outer edges of top and lining layers, enclosing seams. Pin so folded edge of lining butts welting.

8) Slipstitch lining to welting seam by hand. Or edgestitch by machine, using zipper foot; stitch from lining side close to welting.

Padded Headboard

As a finishing touch, a fabric headboard can be coordinated with the bedcover. This is a custom project requiring simple upholstery techniques.

Make a paper pattern template to determine the size and shape of the headboard that will be appropriate to the size of the bed. The headboard should be cut as wide as the bed frame plus allowance for bedding, and 20" to 24" (51 to 61 cm) high plus approximately 20" (51 cm) for legs. Tack the headboard template on the wall behind the bed to check the size and shape. Adjust as necessary.

A shirred border frames the gentle curve of the headboard shown here. Determine the width of the border, approximately 4" (10 cm), and mark template for inner curve.

✂ Cutting Directions

Cut decorator fabric 5" to 6" (12.5 to 15 cm) larger than inner curved section. Cut shirring strip 3 times the measurement of the outer curve and 6" (15 cm) wider than width of shirred border.

For legs, cut fabric the length of leg plus 1" (2.5 cm), and twice the width plus 3" (7.5 cm).

For double welting, cut 3" (7.5 cm) bias strips the length of inner curve, plus extra for finishing.

Use the paper headboard template to cut lining for back of headboard.

YOU WILL NEED

Decorator fabric for front of headboard, for shirred border, and for legs.
Lining for back.
Polyester batting to pad shirred border.
5/32" cording, 2 times the measurement of inner curve.
½" (1.3 cm) plywood, cut to shape; 2" (5 cm) foam to cover headboard; staple gun with ½" (1.3 cm) heavy-duty staples; cardboard stripping the length of inner curve; foam adhesive; white glue.

How to Make a Padded Headboard

1) Cut ½" (1.3 cm) plywood from paper headboard template. Mark template for inner curved section 4" (10 cm) smaller than outer curve.

2) Cut 2" (5 cm) foam even with lower edge and 1" (2.5 cm) larger than headboard curve. Glue to headboard using foam adhesive. To soften edge, pull excess foam to back and staple to edge of plywood.

(Continued on next page)

91

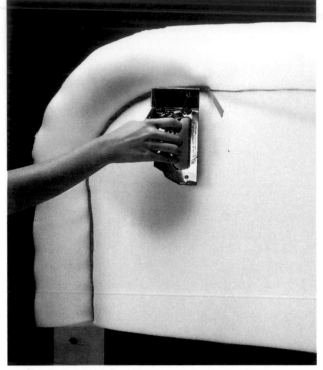

3) Mark inner curve on foam. Staple cardboard stripping on marked line to establish smooth curve. If staples do not penetrate plywood easily, use hammer to tap them in place.

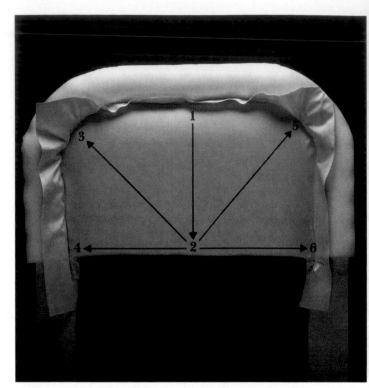

4) Place decorator fabric, right side up, over inner section. Starting at center, smooth fabric taut over foam and staple to cardboard stripping in order shown; then staple every 2" (5 cm). At bottom edge, fold fabric to back; staple. Trim excess fabric.

7) Staple shirring strip to back, easing fabric evenly around curve and forming small tucks as you staple. Keep shirred area an even width on the front.

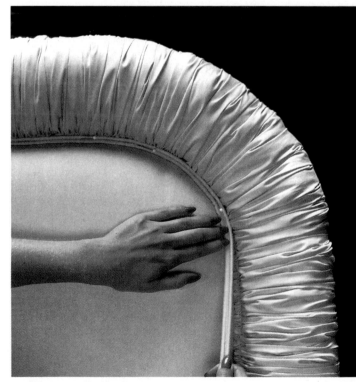

8) Glue double welting (page 113) over stapled area to cover raw edges, stretching welting as you attach it. Secure with pins to hold in place until glue dries.

5) Zigzag over cord to gather one long edge of shirring strip. Divide curve and shirring strip into quarters, and mark. Working from right side, staple gathered edge of shirring to curve, matching marks and adjusting gathers evenly.

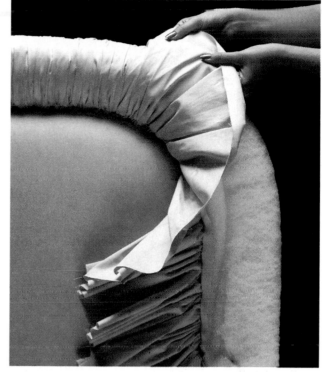

6) Pad border lightly with polyester batting to puff and shape curve. Pull shirred strip to the back.

9) Staple or glue fabric to legs. Press edges of lining under ½" (1.3 cm). Finish back by stapling lining fabric over raw edges.

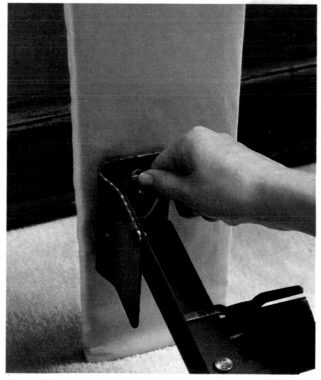

10) Drill holes in headboard to match screws in bed frame. Attach headboard to frame.

Shower Curtains

A simple shower curtain can instantly change and refresh a bathroom. Use the shower curtain as a bold splash of color. Coordinate window treatments, towels, and other accessories with your new shower curtain.

The shower curtain pictured , used with a plastic liner, is especially easy to sew because it does not require grommets or eyelets in the heading. Instead, use a drapery folding or pleating tape, and insert metal shower curtain hooks in the loops that are woven right into the tape. These self-styling drapery tapes can also be used for valances and attached to a flat tension rod with standard drapery hooks.

A valance is a special finishing touch on a shower curtain. It helps to enclose the space and coordinate the room. Most of the valance top treatments used for windows are appropriate shower curtain headings as well. The cloud, pouf, and smocked valances are soft, light treatments; the straight lines of pleated and flat valances are more tailored.

Trim a shower curtain with lace, eyelet, ruffling, or grosgrain or satin ribbon.

✂ Cutting Directions

Cut two 81" (206 cm) lengths of fabric (extra fabric will be needed for matching prints); stitch lengths together. Cut shower curtain 6" (15 cm) wider and 9" (23 cm) longer than vinyl liner.

Cut valance width 2½ times the length of rod, and the desired length plus 4½" (11.5 cm) for heading and hems. Seam together as necessary for desired width. Cut smocking tape the cut width of the valance, plus a little extra for aligning and finishing ends.

YOU WILL NEED

Shower curtain fabric, 4½ yd. (4.15 m) for standard liner; extra needed for matching prints.

Drapery folding tape, 2⅛ yd. (1.95 m) for shower curtain; smocking tape for valance, 2½ times the length of the rod.

Vinyl shower curtain liner, 70" × 72" (178 × 183 cm); 12 metal shower curtain rings; flat tension rod for valance.

Drapery hooks.

How to Sew a Shower Curtain

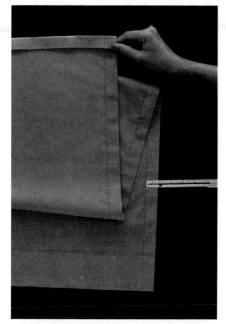

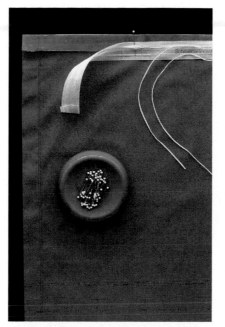

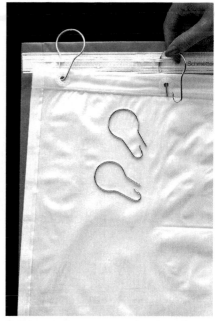

1) Turn under and stitch double 1" (2.5 cm) side hems. At bottom edge, make a double 3" (7.5 cm) hem. At top, press under 1" (2.5 cm). Do not stitch.

2) Remove pull-cords from folding tape. You will use hook loops only. With loop side facing you and toward the top, pin tape on wrong side of fabric ½" (1.3 cm) from upper edge. Turn under raw edge at ends of tape; stitch in place.

3) Insert shower curtain rings into holes of vinyl liner and into hook loops of folding tape. Hang on shower curtain rod.

How to Sew a Smocked Shower Curtain Valance

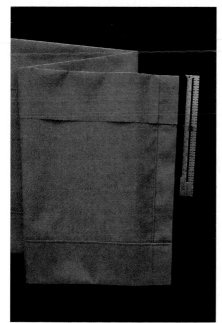

1) Stitch double 1" (2.5 cm) side hems; stitch double 2" (5 cm) bottom hem; turn upper edge under 2½" (6.5 cm), and press.

2) Pin smocking tape ½" (1.3 cm) from upper folded edge with loops on top. Turn under 1" (2.5 cm) of tape at each end, and lift out strings. Stitch both sides of tape.

3) Knot strings securely to prevent them from being pulled out. Pull up strings to smock, adjusting fullness to fit rod. Insert drapery hooks every 3" to 4" (7.5 to 10 cm). Mount flat tension rod; hang valance from rod.

Shower Curtain Ideas

Pouf valance. Make valance (page 54). Mount valance on tension rod. The valance may be mounted at ceiling or just above shower curtain rod.

Eyelet-trimmed curtain. Stitch flat eyelet to curtain in ½" (1.3 cm) seam. Press. Turn under seam allowance; stitch narrow hem.

Box-pleated valance. Use plaid or stripe as guide to make box-pleated valance. Attach separate rod pocket, and cover stitching line with satin or grosgrain ribbon. Mount valance on tension rod.

Cloud valance. Make valance (page 56). Make two shower curtain panels (page 94) to tie back at sides.

Mount curtain panels and valance on tension rods, with plastic liner on installed shower curtain rod.

97

How to Sew a Sink or Vanity Skirt

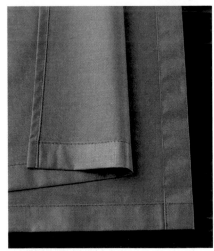

1) Turn under and stitch double 1" (2.5 cm) hem on bottom edge. Turn under double 1" (2.5 cm) hem on center front edges. For 2-piece skirt, stitch narrow hem on back edges.

2) Press under 1" (2.5 cm) on upper edge of panels. Turn under raw edges on ends of shirring tape; pull out shirring cords. Place tape, right side up, over raw edge, with upper edge of tape ¼" (6 mm) from fold. Stitch both sides of tape.

3) Tie cords at both ends of shirring tape. From wrong side of skirt, pull up cords in shirring tape to the finished width. Knot cords; wrap and tuck under skirt. Adjust the gathers evenly.

Sink & Vanity Skirts

For covering up an outdated sink or bringing more fabric coordination into the bathroom, the sink skirt is a perennial favorite. It conceals the plumbing and provides a hidden storage area.

Vanity skirts are sewn the same way as the sink skirt. They can transform an unsightly table into a charming bedroom or bath accessory.

Self-styling shirring tapes, available in a variety of styles, make the sewing quick and easy and add a dimensional interest to the top of the skirt. For a more traditional approach, gather the upper edge (page 106). Attach the skirt to the sink or vanity with hook and loop tape so the skirt can easily be removed for laundering or a quick change. To make the skirt washable, hand-sew the tape in place.

If the sink skirt is attached on the outside porcelain, make two side panels; each panel of the skirt will extend from the center front to the wall. If the skirt is attached underneath the apron of the sink, it can be made in one piece with a center front opening.

✂ Cutting Directions

To finished length, add 3" (7.5 cm) for a double 1" (2.5 cm) bottom hem and 1" (2.5 cm) to turn under at the top. To determine cut width, measure the distance around the sink or vanity where the skirt will be attached; multiply by 2½ times the fullness. Add 4" (10 cm) for front opening hems.

Cut the number of panels as figured above, and seam together for width as needed. If necessary to seam extra widths, place seams toward back.

YOU WILL NEED

Decorator fabric for skirt.

Shirring tape the cut width of the upper edge of the flat panels before gathering.

Adhesive-backed hook and loop tape to go around the sink or vanity.

4) **Finger press** loop side of self-adhesive hook and loop tape to the wrong side of the skirt, over the shirring tape.

5) **Attach** the hook side of self-adhesive tape to the outside of the sink or vanity table. Attach skirt to tape.

Alternative mounting. To hang skirt under apron of sink, attach loop side of tape on right side of skirt ½" (1.3 cm) from upper edge; adhere the hook side of tape to underside of the sink. Attach skirt.

Embellished Towels

Perk up the bath with designer touches added to inexpensive, plain towels. Laces, ribbons, or monograms can be added to coordinate with bedroom sheets and trims, window treatments, and shower curtains.

Preshrink or steam-shrink woven ribbon trims, particularly all-cotton trims; polyester laces will not need preshrinking. Mark trimming placement on towel with water-soluble marking pen.

When applying trims to terry towels, loosen the tension and use a long stitch length. Ease the trimming slightly as you stitch; when the towel is folded on the rack, the trim will lie smooth.

Trimming Ideas for Towels

Lace and ribbon. Trim towels with prefinished lace beading (1), lace edging (2), or galloon lace (3). For lace beading, insert ribbon into beading, position beading on towel, and straight-stitch upper edge. For lace edging, position so lower edge of lace covers towel fringe or hem. Cover upper edge of lace with ribbon trim; straight-stitch along both edges of ribbon. For galloon lace, position trim on towel, and straight-stitch near edges of lace.

Machine monogram. On electronic sewing machine, insert monogram cassette and program desired lettering. Cover monogram area with dissolvable plastic film protector to prevent snagging terry loops. Stitch; tear away plastic film. Laundering dissolves any remaining film.

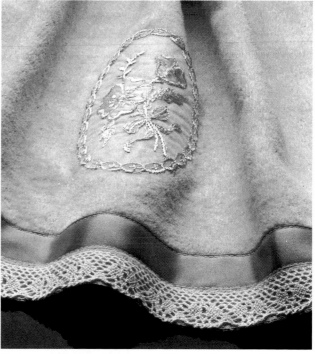

Lace motif. Cut single motif from Cluny or Venice lace, or use purchased appliqué. Fusible web may be used to hold appliqué in place; stitch with narrow zigzag. Coordinating trims may be stitched at lower edge of towel.

Finishing Touches

Accent with Trimming

The addition of a trim may be all that is needed to create a decorator look or embellish a special treatment. Fringe, tassels, braid, silk cord, lace, ribbons, and bows are custom trimmings that add fancy finishing touches throughout the home. Use them on window treatments, valances, and tiebacks as well as on pillows, cushions, and duvets.

Trimmings should be compatible with the mood of the room as well as the weight and care of the fabric. Silky braids and tassels are perfect partners with elegant high-gloss fabrics. Eyelet and lace edgings are essential to a romantic, feminine look. Be sure that washable trimmings are used on washable items.

To mark placement lines for trimmings, use a water-soluble marking pen or a marking pen with lines that evaporate. If pins distort the trim when it is temporarily positioned for stitching, use glue stick to hold the trim in place. If a project lacks interest after it is finished, an applied trim can save it.

Allow extra trim for mitering corners. To be sure that the miter is perfect, you may want to test the trim in place and then baste it in position before stitching, especially when a patterned braid or eyelet needs matching at the corners.

1) Edgings have one raw edge and one finished edge. Lace and eyelet edgings may be flat or preruffled and pregathered. The unfinished edge is stitched in a seam or under a hem. If used on the surface, the raw edge may be covered with a ribbon or braid.

2) Twisted cords are available with an attached woven banding that can be stitched in a seam allowance.

3) Loop fringe has continuous, uncut loops attached to a band heading. The heading may be stitched or glued onto a hem.

4) Tasseled tiebacks are decorative twisted cords with tassels for holding draperies or curtains open.

5) Tasseled fringe has small tufts or tassels attached to a heading. The heading may be stitched or glued onto a hem.

6) Fringe is made of loose strands knotted through a finished heading. The heading may be stitched or glued onto a hem.

7) Ribbons are available in a wide range of colors and widths for every decorative application. Grosgrain is a fine, narrow corded weave. Satin is a smooth weave with sheen. Velvet has dense pile weave on one side. Taffeta is crisp, shiny ribbon with plain, plaid, or moire finish. Ribbons are stitched, glued, or fused onto the surface.

8) Gimp is a narrow decorative braid with a loop or scroll design in one or two colors, used to cover seams and raw edges. It may be glued or stitched in place.

9) Braid has several strands or cords braided together to form a flat surface trim. It is applied on the surface of an item, not in a seam, and is either stitched, glued, or fused in place.

10) Band trims have two finished edges. They are applied the same way as braid.

TRIMMING IDEAS

Tie a wide ribbon and a narrow ribbon of contrasting colors in large bow for tieback or ties on chair seats.

Sew or fuse braid or banding along drapery edges. Use purchased trim, or cut stripes or strips from fabric.

Use flat braid down the sides or along the bottom edge of roller shades.

Use narrow ribbon as bows to tie quilts and comforters.

Apply silky cord on edges of pillows.

Use straight and looped fringe as traditional trims on edges of Austrian valances.

Apply lace on ruffled edges for quick hem on duvets, dust ruffles, and tablecloths.

Sew flat lace or eyelet on edges of pillow shams over solid colors.

Glue or sew braid or banding on edges of lampshades.

Sew six tucks down center of duvet cover; press three each way. Sew a row of lace edging down outside edges of tucks. Repeat on pillow shams.

Three Ways to Gather Ruffles

Zigzag. Stitch ⅜" (1 cm) from raw edge over a strong, thin cord such as string, crochet cotton, or dental floss. Use wide zigzag setting so cord does not get caught in stitching. Pull up cord to gather.

Ruffler attachment. Make a test strip, and adjust ruffler to desired fullness. Measure test strip before and after stitching to determine length of fabric needed. Before ruffling lightweight fabrics, zigzag ⅜" (1 cm) from edge with widest zigzag to give ruffler teeth something to grasp.

Shirring foot. 1) This foot is designed to lock fullness into every stitch, assuring evenly spaced shirring. Set stitch length for a long stitch; the longer the stitch, the greater the fullness. Use balanced tension.

2) Tighten tension, and hold index finger behind presser foot for more fullness with shirring foot. Fabric piles up against finger. Release finger, and repeat until entire edge is gathered.

How to Sew and Attach a Ruffle with a Heading

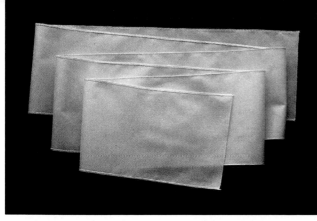

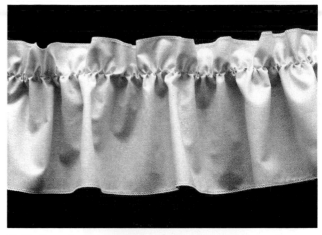

1) Hem both edges of strip to be ruffled with narrow double hem or overlock hem (page 33). Use narrow hemming foot for ⅛" (3 mm) hem.

2) Gather the ruffle strip the desired distance from upper edge, using any gathering technique opposite.

3) Overlock edge, and press ½" (1.3 cm) to right side. Or turn and stitch double ¼" (6 mm) hem on *right* side of the edge where ruffle will be applied.

4) Place wrong side of ruffle on right side of the fabric, with the gathering line on the hemline. Stitch ruffle in place. Allow extra fullness at corners.

How to Apply Ribbon

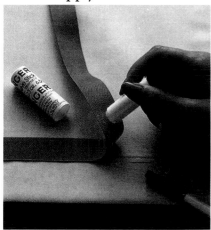

1) Mark trim location, using marking pen with water-soluble or disappearing ink. Use glue stick to hold trim in position.

2) Stitch both sides of the ribbon trim in the same direction to prevent diagonal wrinkles.

How to Apply Braid Trims

Glue a braid trim in place when stitching is not desirable.

How to Miter Corners on an Outside Edge

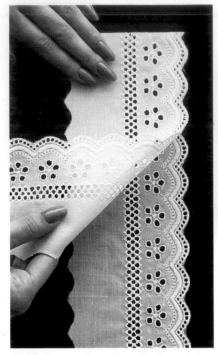

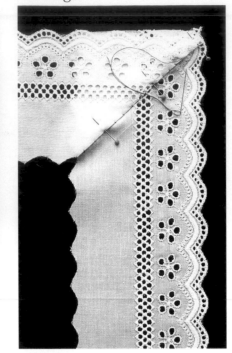

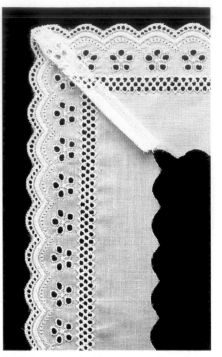

1) Place two lengths of trim, right sides together and edges even. Fold top trim at right angle to form diagonal at corner; press.

2) Slip-baste the two pieces together on the diagonal fold. Unfold trim.

3) Stitch on the line of slip basting on the wrong side. Trim the seams, and finish the edges.

How to Use a Bias Tape Maker

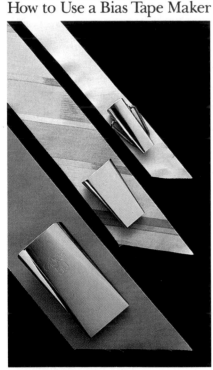

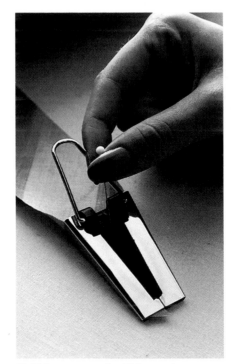

1) Cut bias strip scant 1" (2.5 cm) for ½" (1.3 cm) bias tape; cut 1⅞" (4.7 cm) for 1" (2.5 cm) tape; or 3¼" (8.2 cm) for 2" (5 cm) tape.

2) Trim one end of bias strip to a point. Thread point through wide end of tape maker, bringing point out at narrow end. Insert pin in slot to pull point through. Pin point to pressing surface.

3) Press folded bias strip as you pull tape maker the length of strip. Tape maker automatically folds raw edges to center of strip to create uniform bias tape.

Fabric Rosettes

Use fabric rosettes as decorative accents at the corners of swags and on tiebacks, valances, and balloon table toppers. They need a fairly crisp fabric such as chintz or moire to stand up; in a soft fabric they take on a draped look.

The directions that follow are for a 7" (18 cm) rosette. For a smaller rosette, reduce cutting measurements proportionately. The finished rosette is as wide as the original cut strip.

✂ Cutting Directions
Cut fabric strip 7" (18 cm) wide and 72" (183 cm) long for 7" (18 cm) rosette.

How to Sew a Fabric Rosette

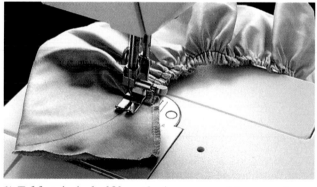

1) **Fold** strip in half lengthwise, *wrong* sides together; gather raw edges; stitch across short ends to round the corners. Trim excess fabric at ends.

2) **Roll** one of the rounded ends tightly toward center to make center of rosette.

3) **Continue** rolling loosely toward opposite end, tacking gathers together with needle and thread.

4) **Shape** "petals" with your hands. Hand-tack rosette in place.

Decorative Welting

Just as piping is used in garments to outline a fashion detail, welting is used in home decorator sewing to define or finish seams. Welting is fabric-covered cording, sewn into a seam to provide extra strength and a decorative finishing touch. Welting is the term used in upholstery and home decorating, and piping is the fashion term; however, the two terms are often interchanged.

Fabric strips for welting may be cut on the bias or the straight grain. For more economical use of the fabric, they are cut on the straight grain. Straight-grain welting is preferred for fabrics that are not tightly woven because bias welting can stretch too much, resulting in an uneven, wavy appearance.

For firm fabrics that must be shaped around curves, bias welting works better than straight-grain welting because it does not wrinkle. Bias welting strips do not have to be cut on the true bias. Cutting the strips at an angle less than 45° gives the flexibility of bias grain but requires less yardage. For stripes and plaids, bias welting does not require matching.

To determine how wide to cut the fabric strips, wrap a piece of fabric or paper around the cording. Pin it together, encasing the cording. Cut ½" (1.3 cm) from the pin. Measure the width, and cut strips to match.

Double welting is glued in place as a finishing treatment to cover seams and raw edges in nonsewn items, such as the edges where two fabrics meet on padded headboards or upholstered walls.

Cording Sizes

5/32" is the usual cording for pillows, cushions, and slipcover seams. Cut fabric strip 1½" (3.8 cm) wide.

8/32" is slightly larger for similar applications. This size is appropriate for gathered welting. Cut fabric strip 1¾" (4.5 cm) wide.

12/32" is jumbo cording that can be used for tiebacks and for decorative finishing. Cut the fabric strip 3¾" (9.5 cm) wide.

22/32" is used for pillows, tiebacks, and tablecloth edgings. It provides weight for a better hang at the bottom of bedspreads and comforters. Cut fabric strip 4½" (11.5 cm) wide.

How to Make and Attach Welting

1) Center cording on *wrong* side of strip. Fold strip over cording, aligning raw edges. Using zipper foot on right side of needle, machine-baste close to cording.

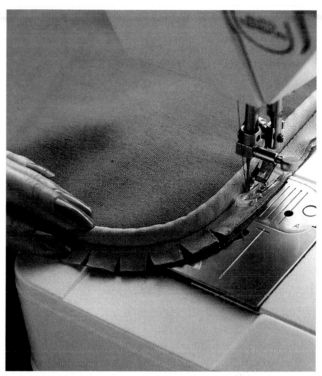

2) Attach welting on right side with raw edges aligned. Begin stitching 2" (5 cm) from end of welting; stitch on bastestitching line. To ease at rounded corners, clip seam allowances to bastestitching.

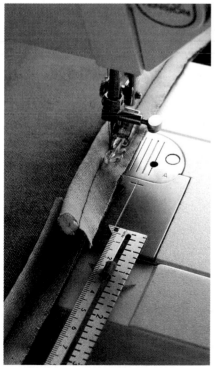

3) Stop stitching 2" (5 cm) from point where cording ends will meet. Leaving needle in fabric, cut off one end of cording so it overlaps the other end by 1" (2.5 cm).

4) Remove 1" (2.5 cm) of stitching from each end of welting. Trim cording ends so they just meet.

5) Fold under ½" (1.3 cm) of overlapping fabric. Lap it around the other end; finish stitching.

How to Make Gathered Welting

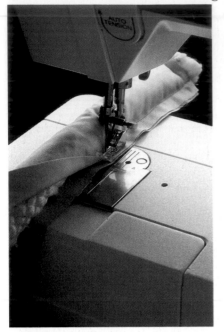

1) Stitch one end of cording to the wrong side of fabric strip. Fold strip around cording, *wrong* sides together, matching raw edges. With zipper foot, stitch for 6" (15 cm) close to, but not crowding, cording. Stop stitching with needle in fabric.

2) Raise presser foot. While gently pulling cording, push fabric strip back to end of cording until fabric behind needle is tightly shirred. Continue stitching at 6" (15 cm) intervals until cording is shirred.

3) Insert pin through fabric strip and cording at end to prevent cording from sliding into strip. Attach gathered welting to item, and join ends of welting as in steps 2 to 5, page 111.

How to Encase Cording

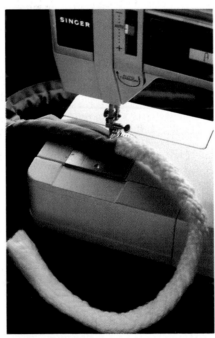

1) Cut cording 2 times the finished length of welting. Cut fabric strip 2" (5 cm) longer than finished length, and width as on page 110. Fold strip around cording, *right* sides together, matching raw edges.

2) Use zipper foot to stitch loosely along cording, from one end of fabric to the other; do not crowd cording. Pivot, and stitch across the cording about ½" (1.3 cm) from edge of fabric.

3) Hold fabric loosely at stitched end; pull fabric from covered to uncovered end of cording, turning tube right side out to encase cording. Cut off stitched end of fabric and excess cording.

How to Make Double Welting

1) **Place** ⁵⁄₃₂" cording on wrong side of 3" (7.5 cm) fabric strip. Fold fabric over cording, with ½" (1.3 cm) seam allowance extending. Stitch with zipper foot next to cording.

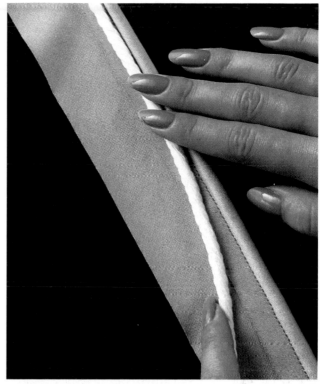

2) **Place** second cording next to first welt. Bring fabric over second cording.

3) **Stitch** between the two cords on previous stitching line. Loosen tension and use zigzag foot riding on top of the welting.

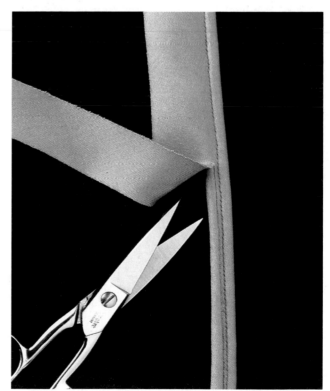

4) **Trim** off excess fabric next to stitching for clean edge finish. Raw edge is on the back of the finished double welting.

Boxed Cushions with Welting

To update any room in the house, make new covers for loose cushions on chairs, benches, or window seats. Boxed cushions may be firm or soft, depending on the foam used. Foam is available in several thicknesses and densities. Use firm or medium density foam for seat cushions; select soft density foam for back cushions. Wrap the foam with bonded polyester batting to keep the cover from shifting and to soften the look of boxed cushions.

Install a zipper across the back of the cover, extending around about 4" (10 cm) on each of the two sides to make it easier to insert the cushion into the finished cover. Or install a zipper across only the back side for cushions that will be exposed on three sides. Use an upholstery zipper, available in lengths longer than dressmaker zippers. The tab of the zipper will be hidden in a pocket at the end of the zipper opening. The concealed tab is an upholstery touch that gives a professional finish to the cushion.

✄ Cutting Directions

Cut top and bottom pieces 1" (2.5 cm) larger than finished cushion size to allow for seam allowances. Cut foam same size as top and bottom pieces for a firm, tight fit. Cut two zipper strips, each the length of the zipper tape; each zipper strip is half the thickness of finished cushion plus 1" (2.5 cm) for seam allowances. Cut boxing strip the length of cushion front plus twice the length of cushion side. Cut welting strips 1½" (3.8 cm) wide, with length 2 times the circumference of the cushion plus seam allowances.

YOU WILL NEED

Decorator fabric for top, bottom, boxing strips, and welting.

Upholstery bonded polyester batting to wrap all sides of cushion.

Foam in desired density and thickness.

Upholstery zipper, about 8" (20.5 cm) longer than back width measurement of cushion.

5/32" cording, 2 times the circumference of the cushion plus seam allowances.

How to Make a Boxed Cushion

1) Measure width and depth of cushion area to determine the size of finished cushion. Determine thickness of foam.

2) Cut fabric and foam. Mark the wrong side of fabric pieces with chalk.

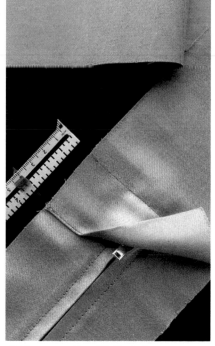

3) Press under ½" (1.3 cm) seam allowance on one long edge of each zipper strip. Position folded edges of strips along center of zipper teeth. Using zipper foot, topstitch ⅜" (1 cm) from folds.

4) Press under 2" (5 cm) on one short end of boxing strip. Lap the boxing strip over the zipper strip to cover zipper tab. Stitch through all layers 1½" (3.8 cm) from folded edge of boxing strip. If desired, edgestitch along fold to within 1" (2.5 cm) of centered zipper.

5) Cover cording, page 111, step 1. Using zipper foot, stitch welting to right side of top and bottom pieces. Stop 1" (2.5 cm) from corner; make diagonal clip to stitching.

(Continued on next page)

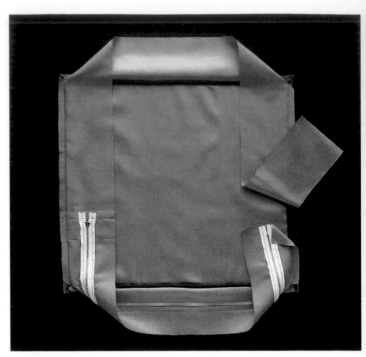

6) Make additional clips as necessary to allow welting to ease around corners. Join ends of welting as in steps 3 to 5, page 111.

7) Place boxing strip on cushion top, right sides together; center zipper on back edge. Start stitching 2" (5 cm) from end of boxing strip, crowding welt. Clip corners as approached; stop stitching 4" (10 cm) before starting point.

10) Place boxing strip and cushion bottom, right sides together. Match clips of boxing strip to bottom corners. Stitch. Turn cover right side out.

11) Wrap cushion with batting; whipstitch in place. Fold cushion to insert in cover. Wrap with plastic to help slide cushion into cover if necessary. Remove plastic.

12) Smooth batting; stretch cover from front to back. Close zipper. Smooth cushion from center to edges. Stretch welting taut from corner to corner to square cushion.

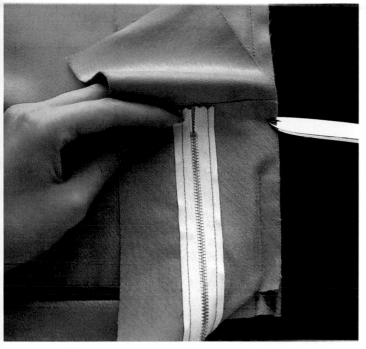

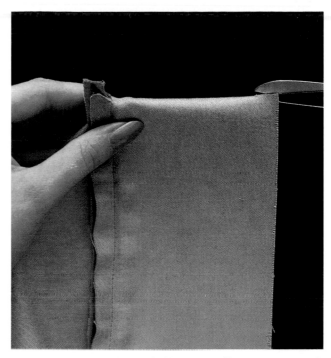

8) Clip to mark seam allowances at ends of boxing strip. Stitch boxing strip ends together. Trim excess fabric; finger press seam open. Finish stitching boxing strip to cushion top.

9) Fold boxing strip, and clip seam allowance to mark bottom corners; be sure all four corners are lined up with cushion top corners. Open zipper.

How to Match Patterns on a Boxed Cushion

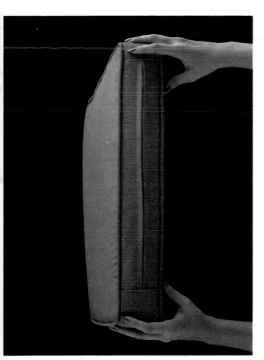

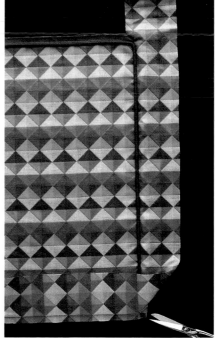

Alternative zipper placement. Install zipper across the back of the cushion, without extending it around the sides, if cushion will be exposed on three sides. The boxing strip may require piecing.

1) Cut cushion top, boxing strip, and bottom to match pattern at front seamlines. For reversible cushion, match pattern from cushion top, down boxing strip, and continue to the back.

2) Notch corners of boxing strip. Join boxing strip to cushion top and bottom, stitching front edge first. Then stitch along other sides of cushion.

Balloon Table Topper

To give basic round tablecloths a custom look, layer them in pairs. Make the bottom cloth floor length, and the top cloth shorter. Although the length of the top cloth is not critical, cutting it one-third or two-thirds of floor length creates a pleasing proportion. For a standard table 30" (76 cm) high, the top cloth should end either 10" (25.5 cm) or 20" (51 cm) from the floor.

Shirr the upper cloth into graceful swags for a balloon topper. To decide the number of swags and the depth to shirr the edge, layer the cloths on the table and pin some test swags in place.

For the fastest hem finish, use an overlock machine to satin stitch the edges or to make a rolled hem. On a conventional machine, apply bias binding or use a hemming foot to sew a narrow hem.

YOU WILL NEED

Decorator fabric for table topper.

Strips of bias tricot or bias tape, equal to number of swags, each as long as the area to be shirred.

Narrow cords such as soutache braid or shade cord, cut twice as long as the area to be shirred plus 1" (2.5 cm). Number should equal the number of swags.

How to Sew a Balloon Table Topper

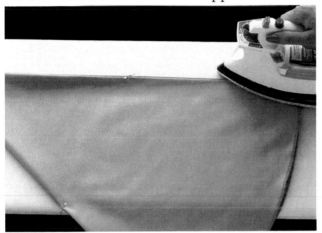

1) Fold hemmed round cloth into quarters, sixths, or eighths, depending on the number of swags. Press crease at each fold to mark desired depth of shirring.

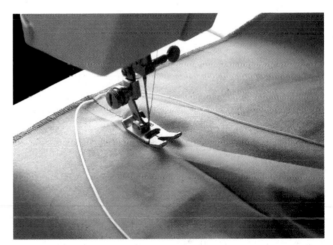

2) Pin doubled cord at hem at each crease. Center bias tricot or bias tape over crease, and pin. Stitch through center of tape, catching cord in stitching at hem edge.

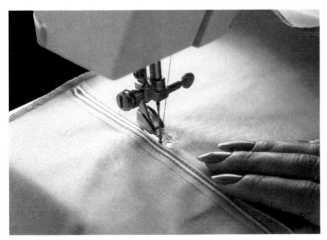

3) Bring cord next to stitching at center of tape. Using zipper foot, stitch along both outer edges of tape to encase cord.

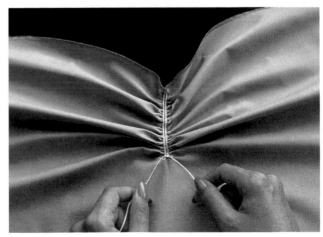

4) Pull up cords to create swags. Adjust gathers, and tie ends of cords securely. Tuck ends of cord into swag; do not cut. Swags can be released for laundry or storage.

Vertical Blinds with Fabric Inserts

To add a practical finishing touch to a contemporary room, vertical blinds are a favorite. For coordination with walls or favorite fabrics and colors in a room, you can create your own vertical blinds with a special type of louver. These blinds have a grooved edge so that matching fabric or wallpaper can be inserted. The technique is simple, and the blinds will cost far less than having it done professionally.

Vertical blinds can be custom-ordered through local distributors. The salesperson can help you determine the correct size and amount of fabric needed.

Select a mediumweight, firmly woven fabric that does not ravel, such as polished cotton, sateen, chintz, or printed sailcloth or sheeting. Avoid fabrics with stripes or diagonal patterns; be aware that the louvers will overlap, causing some distortion of pattern design. Do not use heavy upholstery fabrics or open-weave fabrics that are hard to keep on-grain. If in doubt about the suitability of the fabric, make a test strip to

be sure it fits in the edge grooves. A large, flat work area is essential.

✂ Cutting Directions

Cut fabric 4" to 6" (10 to 15 cm) longer than louver height. Width of fabric required equals the width of each louver times the number of louvers. If more than one width of fabric is required, match design across all widths.

Cut strips of pressure-sensitive tape 1" to 2" (2.5 to 5 cm) longer than louvers.

YOU WILL NEED

Decorator fabric for louvers.

Louvers and mounting hardware; pressure-sensitive backing.

Rubber roller, liquid fray preventer.

How to Insert Fabric in Louvers

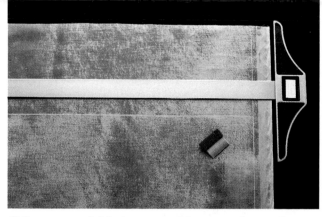

1) **Lay** pressed fabric, *wrong* side up, on large, flat work surface. Draw straight line next to selvage. With T-square, mark crosswise line at top of fabric.

2) **Peel** paper off pressure-sensitive tape for a few inches (centimeters), and align with marked line. Peel paper away, and press tape to fabric for length of strip. Use rubber roller to adhere strip to fabric.

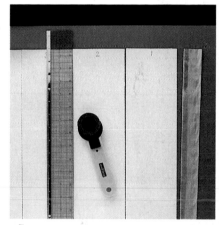

3) **Place** strips next to one another, leaving just enough space between strips to cut apart with rotary cutter or scissors. Press strips firmly in place with roller.

4) **Number** strips with pencil to keep them in order for matching the print. Mark cutting line on strips at right angle to selvage.

5) **Cut** on marked line at top of strips with rotary cutter or scissors. Cut strips apart.

6) **Insert** strips into grooves at edge of the louvers. Trim excess fabric at lower edge; tape is longer than the louvers to allow for fabrics that ravel.

7) **Prevent** slight raveling at upper and lower edges with a light application of liquid fray preventer.

8) **Mount** louvers, following the manufacturer's directions, with numbers in order so pattern matches across width of window.

Fabric Screen

Fabric screens are decorative and functional. A simple screen instantly blocks an unattractive view, fills an empty corner, or separates a conversation or sleeping area. It is also an elegant way to show off an unusual fabric.

Decorative folding screens with removable dowels for mounting fabric panels are available at stores selling unfinished furniture, or you may construct wooden frame panels and hinge them together.

If the fabric has no obvious right or wrong side, such as lace and a woven plaid or stripe, it can simply be hemmed on the sides. Fabrics with an obvious right and wrong side need to be made double or with a contrasting lining, because both sides of the fabric may show.

✂ Cutting Directions

For hemmed panels, measure from top of upper dowel to bottom of lower dowel; add allowance for rod pockets and double headings at the top and bottom. The rod pocket is 2 times the diameter of the dowel.

The cut width of the fabric panel depends on the fabric. Generally, 1½ times the fullness is sufficient and will not distort a print; add 2" (5 cm) to each panel for side hems. Small prints and solids may use more fullness.

For a lined panel, measure from the top of the upper heading to the bottom of the lower heading. Add 1" (2.5 cm) for seam allowances. Cut decorator fabric and lining same size.

YOU WILL NEED

Folding screen with removable dowels for fabric insertion.

Decorator fabric and optional lining, as determined by type of fabric.

How to Sew a Fabric Screen

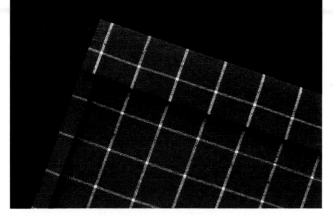

1) Press under double ½" (1.3 cm) side hems. On ends, turn under ½" (1.3 cm), then heading and rod pocket allowance. Stitch side hems, then rod pockets and headings.

2) Slip the dowels into the rod pockets; attach panels to the screen.

How to Sew a Lined Fabric Screen

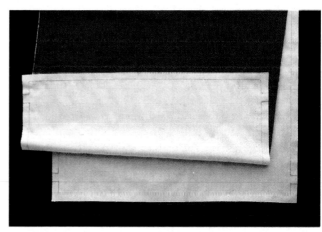

1) Pin right sides of decorator fabric and lining together with all edges even. On the lining, mark the heading and opening for rod pocket, allowing for ½" (1.3 cm) seam at upper and lower edges.

2) Stitch all four sides in ½" (1.3 cm) seam, leaving openings for upper and lower rod pockets on both sides of panel. Leave an 8" (20.5 cm) opening at lower edge for turning right side out.

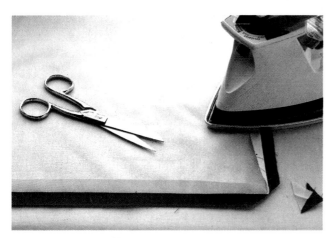

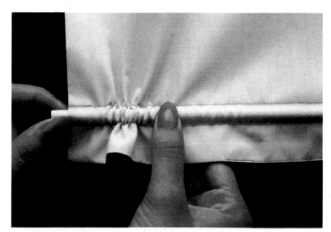

3) Trim corners diagonally. Press lining seam allowances toward lining. Turn panel right side out. Press edges.

4) Stitch rod pockets on upper and lower edges, stitching across panel at opening. Edgestitch the 8" (20.5 cm) opening closed at the lower edge. Slip dowels into rod pockets; attach panels to screen.

Upholstered Walls

An upholstered wall is a dramatic finishing touch that adds a soft, sculptured look to a room. The batting absorbs sound and covers imperfections.

Plaids or stripes will call attention to a floor or ceiling that is not squared. Stripes must be carefully stapled to keep them looking straight. It is easy to staple fabric to wood and plasterboard walls, but staples will not penetrate metal corner pieces. Before starting, remove switch plates and outlet covers. Do not remove moldings or baseboards because double welting will cover fabric edges.

✂ Cutting Directions

Cut fabric lengths as figured in chart, right. Do not trim selvages unless they show through the fabric.

Measure around doors, windows, and ceiling and floor lines to determine the amount of double welting needed. You will also need double welting from floor to ceiling for each corner. Cut 3" (7.5 cm) welting strips equal to this measurement.

YOU WILL NEED

Decorator fabric for upholstered walls.

Staple gun, ¼" (6 mm) staples, ⅝" (1.5 cm) polyester upholstery batting; or ¼" (6 mm) foam; pushpins; single-edged razor blades; hot-glue gun; white glue.

Amount of Fabric Needed

Cut Length	in. (cm)
1) Measurement from floor to ceiling plus 3" (7.5 cm)*	=
Cut Width	
1) Width of fabric minus selvages	=
2) Fabric widths: Width of each wall divided by width of fabric**	÷
Welting	
1) Welting length (see Cutting Directions)	
2) Divided by width of fabric	÷
3) Number of strips times 3" (2.5 cm)	=
Total Fabric Needed	
1) Cut length (figured above)	
2) Fabric widths (figured above) for all walls	×
3) Fabric needed for all walls	=
4) Fabric for welting	+
5) Number of yd. (m) needed: Total width needed divided by 36" (100 cm)	yd. (m)

*Allow extra for pattern repeat; do not subtract for windows and doors unless they cover most of the wall.

**Round up to the nearest whole number.

How to Upholster a Wall

1) Staple batting every 6" (15 cm), leaving 1" (2.5 cm) gap between batting and edge of ceiling, corners, baseboard, and moldings. Butt edges. Cut out batting around switch and outlet openings.

2) Seam fabric panels together for each wall separately, matching motif carefully (pages 30 and 31). Avoid placing seams next to a door or window.

3) Start hanging fabric from top, turning under ½" (1.3 cm) and stapling every few inches (cms). Begin at a corner where matching is not critical. Do not cut around windows and doors.

4) Anchor fabric in corners, pulling taut and stapling close to corner so staples will be covered with welting. Trim excess fabric. Start next panel at corner.

5) Staple along baseboard, pulling and smoothing fabric taut to remove any wrinkles. Trim excess fabric along baseboard with single-edged razor blade.

6) Mark outside corners of windows and doors with pushpins. Cut out openings with diagonal cuts into corners. Turn under raw edges, and staple around molding.

7) Make double welting (page 113). Run hot glue about 12" (30.5 cm) at a time along seam on back of welting. Carefully push welting into position to cover staples.

8) Press welting into corners and around openings. Use screwdriver to force welting into corners. Glue dries in about one minute. After it dries, peel off any excess.

9) Apply fabric to switch plates and outlet covers, using white glue diluted with water. Clip and trim around openings. Turn raw edges to back of plate, and glue.

Index